MINGEI

MINGEI
Masterpieces of Japanese Folkcraft

Japan Folk Crafts Museum

KODANSHA INTERNATIONAL
Tokyo • New York • London

This volume has been published in a soft-cover edition titled *Mingei: The Living Tradition in Japanese Arts* to coincide with an exhibition of the same name. The Mingei exhibition and catalog, part of the UK Japan Festival 1991, were supported through the generosity of the following sponsors: in the United Kingdom, The Royal Bank of Scotland and Sanwa Bank; in Japan, Fuji Xerox, SECOM, Dai Nippon Printing Company, and NTT (Nippon Telegraph and Telephone Corporation). In additions, the Japan Folk Crafts Museum wishes to express its gratitude to the Japan Festival Committee, with offices in Japan and the United Kingdom, for its support.

Photography by Yutaka Seki. Additional photography on front and back jacket and on page 33 by Tsunehiro Kobayashi.

A Brief History of the Japan Folk Crafts Museum, *The Discovery of Beauty*, and Notes to the Plates were translated from the Japanese by Juliet Winters Carpenter.

Mingei: The Word and the Movement was translated from the French by Jules Young.

Distributed in the United States by Kodansha America, Inc., 114 Fifth Avenue, New York 10011, and in the United Kingdom and continental Europe by Kodansha Europe Ltd., Gillingham House, 38–44 Gillingham Street, London SW1V 1HU. Published by Kodansha International Ltd., 17–14, Otowa 1-chome, Bunkyo-ku, Tokyo 112, and Kodansha America, Inc.

The Rise of Mingei copyright © 1991 by Glasgow Museums. *Mingei: The Word and the Movement* copyright © 1991 by Elisabeth Frolet. All other text copyright © by Japan Folk Crafts Museum (Nihon Mingei-kan). English translations copyright © 1991 by Kodansha International. Photographs copyright © 1991 by Japan Folk Crafts Museum.

All rights reserved.
Printed in Japan.
First edition, 1991
91 92 93 10 9 8 7 6 5 4 3 2 1

ISBN 4-7700-1582-8

Contents

Introduction
Sōri Yanagi
7

Mingei: The Word and the Movement
Elisabeth Frolet
9

The Rise of Mingei
Nick Pearce
19

A Brief History of the Japan Folk Crafts Museum
Sōetsu Yanagi
25

The Discovery of Beauty: Sōetsu Yanagi and Folkcrafts
Sōri Yanagi
29

Color Plates
33

Notes to the Plates
169

Acknowledgments
199

Introduction

This book celebrates the simplicity and beauty of Japan's traditional folkcrafts, which are popularly called mingei. Prior to the modern era, handcrafts flourished throughout the country, nurtured by the needs and tastes of the populace. When Japan began to industrialize in the late nineteenth and early twentieth centuries based on western models, local handcrafted work began to fade. Many crafts were in danger of dying out altogether. Distressed at the prospect of factory-made objects replacing handmade ones, Sōetsu Yanagi devoted himself to collecting and preserving mingei and to reawakening his countrymen to the beauty of native folkcraft traditions. With Shōji Hamada, Bernard Leach, and others, he founded the Japan Folk Crafts Museum and eventually succeeded in fostering a new appreciation for mingei, a word he coined to describe this "art of the people." It is because of Yanagi's enthusiasm and commitment that many Japanese craft traditions remain vital today and that countless fine objects from the past have been rescued from oblivion.

Mingei objects are distinguishable from many of the so-called fine arts by their creators' low social status and humble intentions. In general, craftspeople were anonymous, their first priority being to produce something functional. Yet their work displayed a keen sense of design. The Japanese penchant for wanting every facet of their surroundings to be beautiful, including the things they lived and worked with every day, led them to produce seviceable objects that were also pleasing to look at and touch.

Yanagi recognized this special kind of "everyday beauty" in the utilitarian character of mingei, praising such objects because their forms and decoration were not contrived but arrived at unconsciously and intuitively over time. Their designs evolved from practical considerations and long familiarity with materials and accepted shapes, not from egocentric desires. The makers' mastery of material and technique through constant repetition led them to create works with an assurance and spontaneity not always apparent in the fine arts. This natural confidence animates many of the pieces in this volume: the sweeping curves of brass kettles, the freely brushed paintings on Seto ware oil-drip plates, or the boldly conceived paste-resist designs on cotton kimono and bedding. For the most part, mingei are decorated in a straightforward manner, though some can be disarmingly playful and inventive.

A further distinguishing feature of mingei is the reliance on local, natural materials. From ancient times Japanese artisans prized the natural character of the media they were working in. This aesthetic sensibility is apparent in the roughly textured clay bodies and natural ash glazes of such folk ceramics as Tamba—wares that have a warmth and vitality lacking in their more refined, Chinese-influenced counterparts—

and in the wooden pot hangers that have been lovingly planed to reveal the texture and grain of the original tree trunks. A similar love and respect for nature can be found in the other craft traditions as well.

Just as the creators of mingei took pride in their craftsmanship, so we, too, are proud of their achievements. It is hoped that this exhibition and book will continue the mission begun by Sōetsu Yanagi by opening the door of discovery to the beauty of Japan's living folk traditions.

Sōri Yanagi
Director, Japan Folk Crafts Museum

Mingei: The Word and the Movement

Elisabeth Frolet

> *"The coming years will demonstrate that craft will be the salvation of us artists. We will no longer exist alongside the crafts but shall be part of them since we are obliged to earn money. For great art this historical inevitable development is a necessity. All the great achievements of the past, the Indian, the Gothic miracles, arose out of total mastery of craft."*
>
> — Walter Gropius, in a speech given to students during the first exhibition of their work in July 1919.

Japan's ancient artistic culture is renowned for its complexity and refinement, but its much more recent art history is no less remarkable. Art history as a discipline evolved at the end of the nineteenth century with the arrival of Westerners in Japan, particularly Ernest Fenollosa (1853–1908). This learned man, a devotee of the Nō theater who was also extremely interested in Buddhism, was to become a crucial figure in laying the foundations for a historical approach to art that would allow Japan's heritage to be evaluated and classified. However, Fenollosa's work would not suffice to establish all the critical apparatus necessary to analyze the aesthetics of a country whose thought was molded by Buddhism and Shinto rather than by Hellenism.

In the 1920s, the art critic and philosopher Sōetsu Yanagi (1889–1961) appeared on the scene, and to a certain extent he took up where his predecessors Fenollosa and Tenshin Okakura (1862–1913) had left off. Disturbed by the swift disappearance of several traditional art forms as a result of Japan's intense modernization, Yanagi devoted himself to the three tasks of analysis, preservation, and regeneration. After long study, he created several terms that have now become accepted in contemporary Japanese language. The term that particularly concerns us here, and which is also the best known, is "mingei." This word, coined by Yanagi and his two friends Kanjirō Kawai (1890–1966) and Shōji Hamada (1894–1978) in 1925, was destined for an existence both troubled and felicitous. It stirred up passions, and to this day mingei has both its detractors and its supporters.

The term has not always been accepted within contemporary art circles in Japan, and it is still difficult to assess the role of its creator, even though Yanagi was the moving force behind several museums and at least two magazines. At the same time, Yanagi revitalized hundreds of vocations in both Japan and the West. His prolific and eclectic writings cover such diverse fields as the philosophy of Henri Bergson (1859–1941), the poetry of William Blake (1757–1827), spiritual phenomena, Impressionism, Renaissance art, Korean art, Buddhism, the tea ceremony, and, last but not least, mingei.

Sōetsu Yanagi

Kanjirō Kawai

Shōji Hamada

The word "mingei" itself has been used indiscriminately, and in the 1960s and 1970s it became synonymous with objects done in bad taste. However, for Yanagi the word represented the crystallization of his studies on Japanese aesthetics, and as such it cannot be lightly dismissed. The time is now ripe to reevaluate this term and to try to clarify its importance in contemporary Japanese artistic consciousness.

The Meaning of Mingei

Mingei is an abbreviation of the phrase (also invented by Yanagi) *minshūteki kōgei*, or "people's art," and Yanagi defined it as follows:

> Mingei is a new word.... Etymologically, it has the sense of "the art of the common classes." In fact, I conceive it in opposition to the arts of the aristocracy. The functional objects that common people use in everyday life are called *mingeihin*, which can be abbreviated to *minki* (utensils of the people). Objects of daily life—clothes, furniture, tableware, and writing implements—fall into this category.... Mingei consequently have two characteristics: the first is functionality, and the second is ordinariness. In other words, objects that are luxurious, expensive, and made in very small numbers do not belong to this category. The makers of mingei objects are not famous people but anonymous craftspeople.[1]

Yanagi would adhere to this definition throughout his life. He may have at times applied it too subjectively, a laxness on his part that incurred many criticisms.

The Appearance of the Word Mingei

This word was invented in 1925, virtually at the beginning of the Shōwa era (1926–89), which followed on the heels of the Great Kantō Earthquake of 1923 and heralded the arrival of a period with new preoccupations. During this era, Japan's liberalism was tempered, giving rise to important readjustments. Economically, Japan had become a creditor nation for the first time, while politically it proclaimed its imperialist mission. From the viewpoint of the history of thought, many intellectuals reacted against the overwhelming cultural influence of the West. Several members of the avant-garde literary group called Shirakaba returned to native traditions, despite the fact that throughout their youth they had been totally immersed in Tolstoy, Rodin, Balzac, and Schopenhauer. This return swing of the pendulum was predictable in intellectuals initially infatuated with the West, for without it they risked losing their own identities. Such a roundabout path through Western tradition had been necessary in order for them to rediscover the significance of their own culture.

This sudden turning back to native traditions took several forms in Japan. It was particularly pronounced in people who believed blindly the propaganda about the Greater East Asia Co-Prosperity Sphere. In others, it was a cold and cautious decision. Yanagi himself never gave any hint of being party to any military adventures. Although his own return to his Asian roots—first those in Korea and later those in Japan—took place concurrently with the mounting nationalism, he never once adopted any of the current militaristic rhetoric. His creation of the word mingei was, above all, humanistic and aesthetic.

Reasons for Creating the Word Mingei

From 1912 to 1923, Yanagi was busy writing articles on philosophy and art criticism for the journal *Shirakaba*. This avant-garde publication was totally committed to Western literature and painting; its heroes were Tolstoy, Rodin, Renoir, Gauguin, Van Gogh, Goya, and others. Yanagi himself was completely engrossed in books on Medieval Europe, on spiritual phenomena, and on William Blake. He wrote numerous articles about Western art in which he discussed Beardsley, Rodin, Renoir, and—on several occasions—Bernard Leach (1887–1979), who was then teaching etching to several members of the Shirakaba group. However, from 1916, Yanagi found his attention gradually turning toward Korea and its folkcrafts. Influenced in part by Leach, who, with the potter Kenkichi Tomimoto (1886–1963), had thrown himself into ceramics, Yanagi's focus eventually shifted to Asian art.

After six years, his growing fascination with Asian culture led to his conviction that it was time to lessen the emphasis on Western ways of thinking in Japan. Only then could natives look freshly at their own traditions. Yanagi expressed his thoughts

Bernard Leach

in the July 1921 issue of *Shirakaba*: "It is clear that forgetting our own wisdom in order to seek truth overseas was a necessary, if roundabout, route. However, we have now broken the bonds of our own heritage to a sufficient extent to be able to reflect calmly and freely on Asia. We have discovered that we ourselves have an even greater truth, one that has little in common with the morality, religion, and art hitherto taught us by our scholars, monks, and artists."[2] Yanagi was not disparaging the West but merely wanting to reestablish a sort of balance. He felt that this "aesthetic truth" could be found in mingei, but he did not yet possess the necessary elements to fully define the nature of this truth. Several years passed before he could clearly set forth the terms of this new way of creating and looking at art.

How the Word Mingei Was Created

To come up with a term that crystallizes a number of complex ideas is not easy. Yanagi arrived at the word mingei after long and tortuous reflections on Western and Eastern art. Some of the major influences upon him are discussed below.

William Morris and the Middle Ages

In early twentieth-century Japan, there was considerable interest in the thought of William Morris (1834–96), whose historicism was strongly influenced by Gothic art. Yanagi's friends Tomimoto and Leach had shown him this path, and thereafter Yanagi undertook his own research on Medieval European society and the utopian ideals of Victorian England. On the way, he encountered the work of John Ruskin (1819–1900). However, it was William Morris who provided Yanagi with the richest material for the development of his Mingei Movement. Concepts such as the following were of the utmost importance for Yanagi: "Because craftsmen took pleasure in their work, the

Middle Ages was a period of greatness in the art of the common people.... The treasures in our museums now are only the common utensils used in households of that period, when hundreds of medieval churches—each one a masterpiece—were built by unsophisticated peasants."[3]

Yanagi adopted three of Morris's ideas in particular: the value of the art of the common people, which he would translate as mingei; the value of common household utensils, which he would collect and call *zakki*; and the value of the unknown craftsman. ("Country bumpkin" was the term used by Morris.) Other ideas, such as "art made by the people for the people," would also subsequently make their appearance in his theories. Furthermore, from Morris he gained an interest in cooking, which became an occasion for choosing "honest" and "simple" vessels. Yanagi's curiosity was also stimulated by the Arts and Crafts Movement, particularly in relation to peasant and rural architecture.

To underline the surprising correspondences between these two thinkers, one might add that Yanagi and Morris were both creators of numerous new directions in the field of crafts and design.

William Blake and Walt Whitman
Perhaps more surprising is the role of Blake and Whitman in the formation of Yanagi's artistic sensibilities. Yanagi admired Blake's mysticism, his ability to link writing and image, and his propensity to unite opposites—heaven and hell, innocence and experience, life and death. His respect for this poet never left him, even when he was completely bound up with the Mingei Movement. He once wrote to Bernard Leach: "I am sure Blake must be one of the greatest forerunners of modern thought."[4] The Mingei Movement, which promoted the aesthetics of the most humble and unpretentious objects, has echoes of Blake's beliefs and his defense of the "helpless" lamb. The notions of liberty, joy, pleasure, beauty, strength, and innocence all appear in Yanagi's most important writings: *The Way of the Craftsman*, *The Beauty of Everyday Utensils*, and *The Unknown Craftsman*.

The influence of Walt Whitman (1819–92), also a mystic and the spiritual brother of Blake, is found in Yanagi's enthusiasm for popular culture and its wholesomeness. Writing on Whitman in the early 1930s, Yanagi notes: "I could sing the beauty of mingei using [Whitman's] words.... His poems are a revolution.... It is necessary to extol the beauty of the common people themselves."[5]

Asian Cultural Traditions, Buddhism, and the Tea Ceremony
It is obvious that a thinker concerned about the aesthetics of his native country could not limit himself to Western references without incurring distrust. From the end of the 1920s, Yanagi, with his naturally inquisitive spirit, plunged into the study of Asian

cultural traditions. His friend Daisetz Suzuki (1870–1966) acted as a guide, leading him into the world of Buddhist philosophy that had influenced the aesthetics of traditions like the tea ceremony. Buddhism was an important discovery for Yanagi, because it, on the other hand, revealed to him a truly formal and "modern" universe and introduced him to all the semantic material lying within its cultural boundaries. Instead of referring to Rodin, he could talk of the Buddhist deity Miroku Bosatsu[6] and the solitude and tranquillity emanating from him. The terms *sabi* and *wabi*, which describe the reserve, detachment, and frugality apparent in tea-ceremony utensils, were adopted by Yanagi to describe mingei objects of good quality. Similarly, the Buddhist concept of *mu* (nothingness) also entered his vocabulary. He applied it to such features as irregularity, or the absence of the decorative patterns usually seen on Western porcelain. *Mu* also embraced what the Japanese call *shibui*, that aesthetic quality so removed from the perfection defined by Grecian canons of art. In aesthetic terms applicable to mingei, *shibui* represents irregularity, asymmetry, imperfection, and poverty of means. The Asian flavor of Yanagi's mingei theory would grow in strength until it finally obliterated his debt to the West. Almost naturally, his philosophy underwent a process of cultural syncretism, with East and West mixing to such an extent that it became impossible to distinguish the influence of one or the other.

The Nature of Mingei Objects

A visit to the Japan Folk Crafts Museum (Mingei-kan) in Komaba, Tokyo, is undoubtedly the best way to understand mingei. Objects are divided into two categories: traditional ones and those made by contemporary artists/craftsmen. The traditional mingei object must meet the following criteria, as defined by Yanagi: it must be made by an anonymous craftsman or -woman and therefore be unsigned; it must be functional, simple, and have no excess ornamentation; it must be one of many similar pieces and must be inexpensive; it must be unsophisticated; it must reflect the region it was made in; and it must be made by hand.

Contemporary mingei must have the same features except that they are made by artists who are also craftsmen. Bernard Leach, Shōji Hamada, Kanjirō Kawai, Shikō Munakata (1903–75), and Keisuke Serizawa (1895–1976), each in his own field, adapted Yanagi's theories to their creative work. They remind us of the experiments of Morris or of Gropius (1883–1969), who wrote in 1919: "Architects, painters, sculptors, we must all return to crafts! For there is no such thing as 'professional art.' There is no essential difference between the artist and the craftsman. The artist is an exalted craftsman.... Let us therefore create a new guild of craftsmen without the class distinctions that raise an arrogant barrier between craftsman and artist."[7]

Yanagi, unlike members of the Bauhaus, rejected the introduction of machines and

Shikō Munakata.

Keisuke Serizawa

distanced himself from Tomimoto, who became interested in design and its relationship to creativity. But do we have the right to disparage Yanagi's work on the basis of his own rejection of certain aspects of modernity? It is more meaningful, I believe, to acknowledge Yanagi's achievement of having tried to give contemporary Japanese art the first elements of semantic independence. Through words describing characteristic Japanese qualities, the principles of an independent aesthetic eventually evolved. For example, Yanagi promoted the use of words such as *yūgen*, *shibui*, *sabi*, and *mingei*, rather than words borrowed from the West that hampered the understanding as well as expression of native aesthetic perceptions.

By promoting the ideals of mingei, Yanagi attempted to stimulate a creativity that would depart from established canons. He arrived at it through his collection of objects and with the help of the artists around him. Some people might argue that mingei is an anachronism, that it is impossible these days to make great numbers of objects inexpensively by hand, and that the art Yanagi intended for ordinary people is now an art of the elite and not of the common people. Yet it remains to be seen to what extent the craftspeople who fled from the straitjacket of the mingei group and who are active at present (for example, Issey Miyake, Kiyoshi Awazu, Sōri Yanagi, and many others not so well known) will be inspired to produce outstanding works based in spirit, if not in form, on the teachings of Sōetsu Yanagi.

Notes
1. Sōetsu Yanagi, *Mingei yonjūnen* (Tokyo: Iwanami Shoten, 1984), 159.
2. Sōetsu Yanagi, "Kondo no sashie ni oite," in *Shirakaba* (July 1921), 108.
3. Paul Thompson, *The Work of William Morris* (London: Quartet Books, 1977), 244.
4. Sōetsu Yanagi, *Complete Works*, vol. 21 (Tokyo: Chikuma Shobō).
5. Sōetsu Yanagi, *Complete Works*, vol. 5 (Tokyo: Chikuma Shobō), 13.
6. Miroku Bosatsu. He is the successor of Buddha and is usually represented seated on a throne.
7. Walter Gropius, *Manifesto of the Bauhaus* (April 1919).

Japan Folk Crafts Museum

The Rise of the Mingei Movement

Nick Pearce

From the beginning of the seventeenth century until 1853, the year in which the American Commodore Matthew Perry steamed his way into the mouth of Edo Bay, Japan had remained an isolated island nation. Its only contacts with the outside world had been with its immediate neighbors, China and Korea, and to a very limited extent with the Dutch, who were allowed to trade from the island of Dejima in Nagasaki harbor. For most of this 250-year period the Japanese people had enjoyed growing prosperity and stability brought about by the powerful unifying hand of the Tokugawa family. The Tokugawas inaugurated a new era, ending the long period of civil wars and securing power over the whole country, which they ruled under the reestablished title of Shogun from their capital at Edo.

During this period of stability, local craft workshops were established and soon prospered. Most villages had craftspeople making everyday items for local use, but in the cities there were guild systems organized by merchants to produce such things as cotton goods, metalwork, and paper. Some cities specialized in particular crafts; for example, Kyoto became known for its silks and lacquerware. Ceramic production, too, tended to be centered in specific areas where there were good clay deposits, with each region developing special techniques and styles that were jealously guarded.

The 1853 arrival of Americans intent on opening Japan to international trade provided the catalyst to change the nation yet again. It brought to the fore the need for Japan to modernize and adopt the industrial and other techniques of the West. The fate of China in the "Opium Wars" (1839–42) was still very vivid in the minds of Japan's ruling elite, and like China, Japan was in no position to challenge Western military pressure.

From 1854 onward, the ports of Shimoda, Yokohama, Kobe, and Nagasaki were opened for trade, together with other ports on the northern island of Hokkaido. Almost immediately foreign trade increased dramatically, and, under commercial treaties negotiated in 1858 and 1866, there were not only no restrictions, but Japan's tariffs were placed under international control and at a level that constituted unequal competition. Japan's predominantly agrarian economy and handicraft workshops were forced to compete with the machine power and precision of Western industries. With the resultant importation of cheap, machine-manufactured goods and the exportation of currency, Japan's balance of payments suffered and her rural handicraft industries began to be seriously undermined.

It soon became apparent that the Tokugawa regime with its rigid organization was unable to cope with the changing situation. The unity of the political elite began to fracture and, after a short civil war, a powerful faction led by the lords of Satsuma and Chōshū reestablished imperial rule in 1868. This became known as the Meiji Restoration, and Japan began its rapid move toward mechanization and industrialization.

As Japan's tariffs were internationally controlled and could not be raised, one of the new Meiji government's first tasks was to establish more competitive home industries. Most imports to Japan consisted of mass-produced consumer goods that competed directly with local handcrafts. Imported cotton yarn was not only stronger and more uniform than domestic yarn, it was also cheaper. Imported woolens, too, were cheaper and warmer than domestic silks. This was the case with a host of other industries. These imports in turn fostered new consumption habits in Japan, and Western-style dress, food, and other commodities became common, at least in Tokyo.

Changing tastes and cheaper prices offered by imports devastated certain native handicraft traditions, but the increased competition of like-with-like was the only way the Meiji government could respond. European and American industrialists were invited to Japan to establish Western-type factories utilizing mass-production methods, even for ceramics, which hitherto had been handmade. The Japanese government also encouraged the establishment of indigenous industries based on Western models, like the Tomioka spinning mill which mechanized the work that had been in the hands of rural silk producers. In 1878, the Aichi cotton-spinning mill was founded on the same principles, namely, to modernize and intensify cotton production.

By trying to compete with the West in this manner, Japan risked a complete break with its old handicraft traditions. To compound the problem, when the old feudatories were dissolved in 1871 and a prefectural system established, local allegiances and traditional methods of distribution were disrupted. The centralization of the developing factory system and its mechanized division of labor also separated craftspeople from all the creative processes that handcrafted production had provided. What crafts survived did so due to the European vogue for "all things Japanese," which reached a high demand by the end of the nineteenth century. Ceramics, ivory carvings, cloisonné enamels, and lacquer all found favor as export commodities. However, designs for these export wares were not based on the traditional utilitarian objects made by local craftspeople. Rather, they were derived from the highly decorated luxury items produced for the court and aristocracy, items that appealed to gaudy Victorian taste. This eclecticism soon found favor in the domestic market, thus compounding the shift away from the original conception of folk crafts. The term "craft" (*kōgei*) soon came to mean "industrial technology."

In many ways, the adoption of Western technology and ideas by Japan was only superficial. Many essentially feudal social patterns and values survived. It was probably this undercurrent of tradition that helped those craftspeople still operating in rural areas to coexist, if only on a limited scale, during the period of intensive industrialization from the end of the Sino-Japanese War (1894–95) to the beginning of the First World War and the Taishō period (1912–26). During these three decades, large-scale labor-intensive industries, ranging from shipbuilding and iron and steel, to paper and ceramics, operated alongside the small family workshops.

The heavy industries received a boost during the First World War when Japan was involved in supplying munitions to the allied armies and goods to the Asian mainland. Between 1914 and 1931, Japan's industries expanded to such an extent that the value of industrial production overtook that of agriculture for the first time in its history. This period also saw the expansion of *zaibatsu* (financial oligarchs), the Japanese system of family-controlled business conglomerates.

It was amidst this intensive period of industrialization that Sōetsu Yanagi and two friends, the potters Shōji Hamada and Kanjirō Kawai, founded the Japan Folk Crafts Association (Nihon Mingei Kyōkai) in 1926. The purpose of the association was to preserve the accumulated knowledge of generations of craftspeople and to promote traditional crafts in the modern age. Those in the association (and the founders were soon joined by like-minded craftspeople) also sought to promote and continue in their own work traditional styles and techniques. Overwrought finesse was not their aim, but rather the functional simplicity of items used in everyday living. Because the traditional term *kōgei* had been hijacked by the newly emerging industry to refer to industrial products, the association had to coin a new word or words to characterize traditional folkcrafts. Thus the term *minshūteki kōgei* (people's art), which was abridged to mingei, was born.

Sōetsu Yanagi was the guiding spirit, the philosopher of the association, much in the way William Morris had been for the Arts and Crafts Movement in England during the previous century. In fact Morris was a direct primary influence on Yanagi, who in many ways shared a similar background and development.

Yanagi was born to a wealthy family in Tokyo and was educated at the Peers School and Tokyo Imperial University, where he graduated with a degree in Western philosophy. As with Morris, one of Yanagi's earliest literary influences was the visionary poet and painter William Blake; in 1914 Yanagi published the first major study in Japanese regarding Blake's life and work. Like Morris, Yanagi also drew round him a group of like-minded friends who were interested in Western arts and philosophy. Morris's group, known as "the Brotherhood," was formed to discuss art, theology, medieval poetry, and the writings of Tennyson and Ruskin. Yanagi's coterie was formed for a more tangible purpose: the publication of a monthly art magazine, *Shirakaba* (White Birch), with the aim of introducing Western art, literature, and philosophy to Japan.

Sometime around 1917 Yanagi's focus started to shift toward a greater appreciation of Asian culture, initially that of Korea, but soon to be followed by a study of traditional Japanese crafts and Buddhist thought. By the time of the formation of the Japan Folk Crafts Association in 1926, Yanagi had formulated most of the aims and ideals of the Mingei Movement.

Many of these aims and ideals originated from his study of traditional Eastern culture, but Yanagi also absorbed many ideas from Western philosophy and art. It is interesting to trace some of these influences, if only as a means to put the origins of the Mingei Movement into their proper context. The importance of William Morris has already been mentioned; it is to Morris that Yanagi can be likened in terms of basic aims—the reevaluation and preservation of traditional craft practices—and in the way the two figures provided the philosophical foundations for their respective movements and gathered round them groups of forward-looking disciples. Although Morris was very much an active craftsman himself while Yanagi remained a theoretician, both relied on the talented artists of their movements. For Yanagi these were Hamada, Kawai, Serizawa, Munakata, and the British potter Bernard Leach, who was one of Yanagi's earliest mentors.

The comparison of Yanagi with Morris, however, should not be taken too far. Morris was essentially an early theoretical influence, as William Blake had been an early spiritual one. Morris's famous dictum "Have nothing in your home that you do not know to be useful or believe to be beautiful," could easily have been written by Yanagi. Likewise Morris's insistence on simplicity, honesty, respect for materials and processes, and the sheer joy of handiwork, was at the core of Yanagi's philosophy. But Morris's move toward politics and socialism was never followed by Yanagi, whose traditional Japanese background favored a far more spiritual path that imbued the thing made as well as the maker.

Yanagi's study of Zen Buddhism provided much of this spirituality, and Zen influence is apparent in many of his writings. He constantly speaks of the spontaneous and the anonymous. He eschewed intellectual analysis in the creative process, stressing that a craftsman who was comfortable with his medium made things freely and spontaneously, his traditional skills guiding him to make simple, useful, and beautiful objects almost effortlessly. In *Mystery of Beauty*, Yanagi wrote: "Korean pots were made not by intellectual analysis, but by a natural and spontaneous attitude of mind."[1]

As Elisabeth Frolet has pointed out, Yanagi's ideas on spontaneity may have Western as well as Asian origins.[2] The writings of the French philosopher Henri Bergson, whom Yanagi read during the years when he was formulating his ideas, contain concepts that are very close to Zen and to Yanagi's beliefs surrounding the creative process. Bergson argued that reality was a continuing stream of change whose impulse is apprehended only by intuition and not by intellect. This equates with Yanagi's "spontaneous attitude of mind." As Yanagi wrote in 1952:

> One who has a chance of visiting a Korean pottery [studio] may notice that the wheel used for throwing pots is never exactly true. Sometimes it is so crudely set up that it is not even horizontal. The asymmetrical nature of Korean pots comes partially from the uneven movement of the surface of the wheels. But we must understand that Koreans do not make such wheels because they like unevenness and dislike evenness, but they just make their wheel in that happy-go-lucky way. Their unevenness is but a natural outcome of the untrammeled state of their minds. They never concern themselves with either this or that but just make wheels. They live just as circumstances permit without any sense of artificiality. Of course if the wheel slopes too much they may correct it to some extent, but that will not mean precision even then. They hardly trouble about accuracy or inaccuracy. They live in a world where accuracy and inaccuracy are not yet differentiated. This state of mind is the very foundation from which the beauty of the Korean pots flows out.[3]

This subjection of the self was also applied when it came to the signing of work. "Signing one's name on one's goods is not wrong," wrote Yanagi, "but from the viewpoint of Oriental religion, it reveals a relative deed of attachment. He signs because he advertises himself through his goods."[4] Here Yanagi stresses not only the Zen denial of the self, but also the tradition of Japanese craftspeople not to sign their works. "When someone asked Kawai: 'Why do you not sign your name on your work?' " wrote Yanagi, "he said: 'My work itself is my best signature.' "[5]

At the same time Yanagi was developing his ideas on the position of craftspeople in the machine age, Walter Gropius in Weimar, Germany, was outlining his ideas on the future of craftsmanship, which he set down in the Bauhaus proclamation of 1919. It is interesting to speculate whether the two knew of each other, as there are striking similarities in their language and their aims. The early Bauhaus philosophy, which lasted until 1923, made as its central axiom the Morrisian view of inspired craftsmanship, with the stress on learning by doing rather than by reading or theorizing. There was also a belief in the unity of the artist and the craftsman, a very Japanese concept where traditionally there was no distinction between fine and applied arts. In the West, a false division had been created which the Bauhaus Proclamation aimed at removing: "There is no essential difference between the artist and the craftsman. . . . Let's create a new guild of craftsmen, without the class-snobbery that tries to erect a haughty barrier between artist and craftsman."[6]

Later, after 1923, the Bauhaus moved away from this emphasis on the paramountcy of the craftsman, and the early ideals of the proclamation did not survive the Second World War. Morris and the Arts and Crafts Movement in Britain had an equally short-term impact, surviving in an undiluted fashion only to the First World War in the guise of such groups as the St. George's Art Guild, the Art Workers Guild (founded by C.F.A. Voysey), and the Guild of Handicrafts (founded by C.R. Ashbee). However, the Mingei Movement seems not to have lost any of its impetus, owing to Yanagi's tireless efforts at promoting it and its ideals and the establishment in 1936 of the Japan Folk Crafts Museum devoted to traditional and contemporary folkcrafts.

Yanagi's ideas also found acceptance abroad. Mention has already been made briefly of Bernard Leach, the British potter born in Hong Kong who went to Japan in 1909 and studied with Kenzan VI, and who soon became closely associated with Yanagi and the emerging Mingei Movement. In 1920, Leach, accompanied by Shōji Hamada, went to England and established the now famous and influential pottery center at St. Ives in Cornwall. The inspiration of traditional Chinese, Japanese, and Korean ceramics, together with the fused ideas of Yanagi and Morris, provided the driving force for Leach and Hamada, and in their wake, inspired generations of studio potters up to the present day. Leach in particular was, like Yanagi, a prolific writer and became the prime mover in England of the Craft Movement. In fact it was Leach who translated Yanagi's book *The Unknown Craftsman* into English and was largely responsible for introducing the concept of "mingei" to the West.

Remarkably, in Japan Yanagi succeeded in arresting the growing decline in craft traditions. He not only engineered a reassessment of Japan's traditional crafts, but he also laid the foundation for modern-day craftspeople to work and serve society in the industrial and post-industrial age. Above all, it was because Yanagi tapped a tradition which was a strong and unbroken one in Japanese society that the Mingei Movement survived its prophet and achieved the wide and high degree of success which continues to this day.

Notes
1. Sōetsu Yanagi, *Mystery of Beauty* (Tokyo: 1952), 26.
2. Elisabeth Frolet, "Yanagi Sōetsu Et Son Mouvement D'Art Populaire, Le Mingei Undo," *Gazette des Beaux-Arts* (Paris: February 1987), 86–96.
3. Yanagi, *Mystery of Beauty,* op cit., 24–25.
4. Sōetsu Yanagi, *The Responsibility of the Craftsman* (Tokyo: 1952), 17.
5. Yanagi, op cit., 19.
6. Quoted from Walter Gropius "Bauhaus Proclamation," in Reyner Banham, *Theory and Design in the First Machine Age* (London Architectural Press, 1960), 277.

A Brief History of the Japan Folk crafts Museum

Sōetsu Yanagi

On January 10, 1926, we[1] were winding up a journey through the Kii area (Wakayama Prefecture) with a visit to the monastery on Mt. Kōya. That very night we decided to construct a folk crafts museum, staying up late and talking the idea over with excitement. Much time had already gone by before we arrived at this decision. All of us were attracted by the beauty of handmade objects, and we had the good fortune to share a common viewpoint. But our judgments differed greatly from those of most people. We often came upon what seemed to us beauty of the highest order in things that others had cast aside, and felt a lack of beauty in what others universally praised. For whatever reason, objects made for daily use aroused our strongest interest and admiration. Certainly we did not have any such preconceived theory of beauty. Our only stratagem was to look at things honestly and straightforwardly. Seeing before knowing is precisely what led us to this marvelous revelation. We wanted to share the joy of our discovery with others, to tell, through objects, of a forgotten beauty.

A similar conviction had led us earlier to build a folk crafts museum in Korea. That was a small-scale venture, but it had provided invaluable experience. Now, inspired by that success, we felt the need for such a museum in Japan, too.

What would we collect for such a museum? All the artifacts would share a certain characteristic. To describe them, we sorely needed a new word, and invented one: *mingei*, meaning folkcrafts, or craftworks created by ordinary people for use in their daily lives. We made no claim that beauty resided in such objects and nowhere else. We simply were satisfied that within them lay a beauty all the more astonishing for its neglect. And we felt that objects connected to people's lives formed the mainstream of craftwork. In this way we formulated plans for a *mingei-kan,* or museum of folkcrafts. It was a task that no one else seemed likely to undertake. Nevertheless, we were certain that such a museum would be of the deepest significance for the history of mingei, for aesthetics, and for the future of manufactured goods. Like converted priests, newly awakened to the world of faith, we vowed to devote ourselves unceasingly to this realm of beauty.

How the museum was to be realized, how much money it would require, how it would be administered, and how maintained—we were far too enthusiastic over the idea itself to worry over such matters. Looking back now, our plans seem to have been poorly thought out, but without the pure, blazing ardor of youth, the work would never have gotten underway at all. Fortunately, we began out of conviction. Our eagerness to move ahead knew no qualms. Had we felt the least apprehension about what might lie ahead, our courage would no doubt have at some point failed.

Our journeys of collecting began. Letting no opportunity slip by, we traveled around the country in search of objects. This was a good many years ago, when the situation was not what it is today. Many antique dealers had never even heard the colloquial word *getemono* (folk wares). Nor was the term "mingei" yet in use. Wherever we went, accordingly, was virgin territory. We had no way of knowing what might turn up, a fact which only increased the pleasure of the hunt. Many of the items we found were buried away, covered in dust. To our great pleasure, we were able to acquire them for a song.

We were more determined than ever to present the fruits of our forays to the public, and so, starting on June 22, 1927, for five days the first exhibition of folkcrafts was held in Ginza. The underlying purpose was to share our view of folkcrafts through the objects themselves. In many ways it was an unprecedented sort of exhibition. Not a single item was signed. All of the work had been created by nameless artisans. None of the objects had much value attached to them, yet they spoke eloquently of beauty.

The exhibition served both to defend and to develop a world that had had no previous recognition. We sought to amend traditional ways of looking at things and to demonstrate a new standard of beauty. We wanted to speak candidly to large numbers of people about the wholesome beauty we saw. Some visitors apparently thought our views biased and eccentric, but we were confident we had found the essence of beauty; to protect and enhance it was our mission.

There was not a shadow of doubt among us that the construction of a folk crafts museum would have deep meaning and value. Still, time passed by without our plans coming to fruition. At that time preparations were under way for the reconstruction of the Tokyo Imperial Museum. Famous museums the world over had a number of rooms set aside for native folk art, and there seemed no reason why our country shouldn't do the same, especially with the wealth of materials at hand. The need for such a facility would no doubt grow more acute. We considered donating our collection to the new museum and sought an interview with the director. But for whatever reason, whether our intentions were not sufficiently well conveyed, or whether there were not enough rooms, nothing ever came of it. This failure, however, only increased our determination. We decided to do the job ourselves, to wait expectantly for the day of fruition. Little by little, poor as we were, we went on adding to our stock of items.

In the summer of 1929, we sat on a hill in Skansen, Sweden, engaged in a discussion. The Nordiska Museet (Nordic Museum) of Stockholm is truly the world's finest museum of rural life. Within its vast, distinctive structure lie tens of thousands of artifacts. It is a splendid, physical tribute to the beauty expressed by Nordic people in woodworking, metalworking, dyeing and weaving, and pottery. Its rooms are set up just like rooms of long ago, as if people were still living in them. This exhaustive and scrupulously organized collection owes its existence to the lifelong labors of a pioneer named Artur Hazelius (1833–1901), who loved, protected, and sought to preserve the products of rural people. His labors involved many trials and tribulations, but in the end they were rewarded. Now the whole country protects his achievement with unending appreciation, and as a result of Hazelius's work, the world has taken greater note of Sweden. Our own trip to Europe was prompted in part by a desire to visit the Nordic Museum.

We considered modeling our museum after this one, but rejected the idea, feeling that we had our own road to travel. Nevertheless, seeing this amazing museum filled us with fresh excitement. We resolved not to strive for quantity, but quality and refinement. We would be severe in our winnowing, basing our judgments strictly on aesthetic values. No collection of anything, anywhere, by anyone, would rival ours in sheer beauty.

More exhibitions and a few slender catalogs seemed to spark a movement of sorts. Gradually, here and there, people began taking note of the articles we had collected. There were those who jeered at us for being bargain hunters, for being so poor that we gave trifles the name of beauty, but across the country, antique dealers with a sharp eye for profits saw a future in such "trifles," and began quickly to make their moves. In particular, the folk crafts exhibition held in Tokyo and Osaka in 1930 under the sponsorship of the Yamanaka Company fueled this trend. Following that exhibition, major department stores began vying with one another to stage similar shows; the new word "mingei" was on everyone's lips, and even became a dictionary entry. The movement was warming up.

The ten years since we initially set forth our goals had flown by with amazing speed. Although in retrospect it seems our efforts may have lagged at times, we were blessed with unwavering faith. Finally, others also became convinced of the need for a museum. On May 12, 1935, we received a visit from the wealthy businessman Magosaburō Ōhara, who offered to donate the funds necessary for the construction of a folk crafts museum. Mr. Ōhara was well known for his contributions to various social welfare projects. We had no words to thank him for his boundless munificence. The task that we had so long set ourselves was about to be realized. We gathered together others who shared our purpose and began to lay concrete plans.

First we decided on the location, and signed a contract for a plot of land at 861 Komaba, in Meguro, Tokyo. Next we determined that the architecture would be traditional Japanese in style and make liberal use of *ōyaishi*, a greenish stone found in Utsunomiya. The foundation was laid in October 1935. Building began and, in addition, a striking stone-roofed rowhouse and gate were transported from Tochigi Prefecture and reconstructed on the premises. There were plans to add more display rooms, a library, an office, a lecture hall, and workshops. As construction proceeded, we continued to collect books and objects in every field and were able to obtain many fine artifacts. After the building was finally completed, the collection was organized and a display was set up. The museum finally opened its doors on October 24, 1936.

1. Four men, with Yanagi, led the Mingei Movement from its start: the British potter Bernard Leach and the Japanese potters Kenkichi Tomimoto, Shōji Hamada, and Kanjirō Kawai.

The Discovery of Beauty: Sōetsu Yanagi and Folkcrafts

Sōri Yanagi

For my father, Sōetsu Yanagi, collecting craftwork was a lifelong passion. I once asked him when he began, and learned that it was while he was in junior high school. He may have inherited the love of collecting from his own father, Narayoshi Yanagi, a man who was not only a noted mathematician and the first director of waterways in the Naval Department, but a collector of everything from works of art and naval materials to cookbooks.

Sōetsu's interest wasn't always focused exclusively on craftwork. As a member of the literary coterie Shirakaba in his twenties, he was eagerly involved in introducing the art of European painters such as Van Gogh, Beardsley, and Cézanne to the Japanese public. In my earliest memories, his interest was apparently divided equally between crafts and European art. Our house in Abiko, Chiba Prefecture, was filled to overflowing with books, reproductions of paintings by Blake and Beardsley, and countless craftworks, along with oil paintings by Cézanne and statues by Rodin for the new Shirakaba Art Museum.

He was also very particular about the dishes we used at home, and wouldn't let us children wear any clothing that he hadn't personally approved. I remember my acute embarrassment at being the only child with bobbed hair (back then all boys had their hair shaved off), and at being forced to wear a red sweater over my clothes.

Sōetsu had strong principles where his own intuition of beauty was concerned. He cared not the least for received standards of beauty, but about what he himself felt to be beautiful he cared passionately. His encounter with Korean Yi Dynasty (1392–1910) ceramics was typical. On being shown a blue-and-white bowl owned by Noritaka Asakawa, who studied ceramics in Korea while teaching there, Sōetsu was so impressed that from 1916 on he made repeated trips to Korea. The peninsula was then under Japanese colonial rule, with no one to speak out in defense of local crafts or culture. Incensed at the injustice of this, Sōetsu founded a museum of Korean folk art in Seoul to encourage Koreans to take pride in their native culture. Later, discovering rough-hewn Buddhist statuary carved by the Japanese monk Gogyō Mokujiki (1718–1810), he was again profoundly moved. Sōetsu traveled around Japan on foot in search of images, becoming so engrossed in the subject that he founded a journal devoted to Mokujiki.

From 1924 to 1933, while living in Kyoto, Sōetsu haunted the flea markets at Tōji and Kitano Shrine in search of folkcrafts to add to his growing collection. He would pick up treasures for a song, including pieces of ragged cloth he found by poking in piles of used clothing with his cane. Mother, who had to launder them, used to balk at the smell, but that is how my father discovered Tamba cloth. Sometimes, when walking in a cemetery, he would see an attractive ceramic dish being used as an incense holder, and be overcome with longing for it. In good conscience he could not simply help himself, so he would unobtrusively replace it with a new one. No one else was interested in folk wares back then, so they cost next to nothing, and in no time he had amassed an enormous collection. Soon we were eating off nothing but folk pottery; finally we even ran out of room to sleep and had to move into larger quarters.

Whenever Sōetsu found something new he would become very excited, summon Kanjirō Kawai or Shōji Hamada, and stay up all night talking over his discovery. I sometimes wonder if anyone else has ever felt such pure joy at beauty or its discovery. That passion was doubtless what drove him to set off on trips across the country, to pore over available literature, and to study the items in his collection with such extraordinary energy.

Gradually, as he went on collecting craftwork and learning all he could about it, Sōetsu became conscious of the special beauty of folk art, and slowly his philosophy of mingei took shape. Interestingly, during that same period Picasso was drawn to African primitive art, and the Bauhaus Movement was occurring in Germany; all over the world, in fact, people were searching for new standards and new forms of beauty. Such a trend may have been motivated in part by second thoughts over the process of modernization; that Sōetsu began lauding folk art just as the production system was in transition from handcrafts to "machine crafts" suggests a rebellion against the shoddy quality of most machine-made goods and nostalgia for the warmth of the handmade goods produced in the premodern era.

But Sōetsu also had serious doubts about the value of the fine arts, or art for art's sake. He aroused enmity by scorning works of art that critics praised and the public flocked to see, attacking them openly in the newspaper. His opinion of purely decorative craftwork such as elegant *maki-e*—paintings in gold dust on lacquerware—was much the same. Even if one or two works produced in isolation happened to be beautiful, unlike folkcrafts, they were not deeply connected with people's lives. To Sōetsu, the issue was this: why should works produced in large quantities by unknown craftspeople for utilitarian purposes, with no particular aesthetic goals in mind, in fact be so beautiful? He concluded that true beauty grew out of the daily lives of ordinary people. In that sense Sōetsu's way of thinking had much in common with the dictum of modern designers that "design is for all people."

The Mingei Movement succeeded in establishing a renewed respect for crafts; yet as modernization progresses, traditional folkcrafts are rapidly disappearing everywhere, not only in Japan. Cost considerations effectively drive handmade goods out of the market. But no sooner does that happen than the warmth and appeal of folk art objects recapture people's hearts, creating a renewal of interest. What was formerly true folk crafts, objects designed to serve a specific purpose, degenerates into baubles made solely to give pleasure, mere souvenirs—a far cry from the nature of mingei as defined by Sōetsu. Or again, folk wares may acquire such market value that their owners shut them carefully away, never using them, in which case they scarcely deserve the name of "mingei" any more. If an object is made not anonymously but as an expression of the maker's individuality, and if it is made not for utilitarian purposes but for purely aesthetic ones, then it ceases to be handcraft for the masses, crossing over rather into the realm of fine art.

In that sense, the modern successor to mingei is design. Like craftspeople, designers produce practical works for all people; the difference is that their products are not handmade, but machine made. Unfortunately, it does not appear that present-day design is truly following the mingei tradition. In order to speed the turnover of goods, designers chase after fleeting fashions and produce objects with flashy, eye-catching appeal. As in post-modern design, they seek after a beauty at such odds with functionalism that much of their output is a total denial of traditional concepts of beauty.

In the words of Sōetsu, the beauty of folk crafts is the beauty of "naturalness and health." It is not created by conscious intent, but is spontaneous, unconscious, and vigorous, arising out of devotion to function. Nowadays, it seems that the greater the part played by designers, the less inspiring the result. True beauty springs from anonymous design such as that of the baseball, where two strips of leather are sewn together with a single seam. The seam is part of the design, yet at the same time it provides the necessary grip for fastballs and curves. The function of being thrown and rolled determines the form of the ball; use equals beauty.

William Morris, the nineteenth-century champion of craftsmanship, said, "Healthy beauty resides in a healthy society." Things reflect the society that made them. For beautiful things to be made, not only the makers but the users and the entire distribution network between must be healthy. That so many products of the Edo period (1600–1868) are beautiful is a sign of the general health of the age. At the same time, there was, I believe, a special rapport or *gemeinschaft* between users and makers.

As an industrial designer, I believe in principle that it is possible to create machine-made products, even tableware and furniture, no less beautiful than those of the age of handcrafted work. And yet there is something in the cultural products of societies where handcraft is a way of life that modern designers cannot match. The magical, raw power of African masks, for example, is beyond the reach of modern city dwellers. In Tibet, men and women call loudly back and forth from atop high peaks, their voices resounding beautifully amid the encircling mountains in a musical dialogue of love. In Mexico, as women thresh wheat with their bare feet, along comes an old man who fashions reeds into a rough flute and begins to play, the women quickly picking up the rhythm with their footsteps. The sound is not polished but earthy, as if it arose from the very soil. This sense of human warmth, born out of daily life and experience, wrung out of the depths of human existence, is missing in modern design.

I believe that beauty is inseparable from *yō*, meaning function or use. *Yō* in the sense that Sōetsu used it is broader in scope than the functionalism and practicality of which modern designers speak. It is a word that embraces the mental or spiritual dimensions of human life. What startles us today when we look at older folkcrafts is the sense of the wellspring of human life that lies within them, from which an innate beauty rises.

The loveliness of handcrafts should be preserved, and to that end I believe it is important to plan for the protection and nurturing of folk crafts. One way to do so is to adapt objects for new purposes, such as using jars for vases and umbrella stands. Handcrafted paper pasted on Chinese baskets provides wonderful indoor lighting. Simply because handmade goods may be beautiful, however, it does not follow that we can or should turn out identical goods on machines. Now that the vast majority of everyday items is machine made, the thing to do is not to insist on a return to the past, but to look to improvements in machine production as the keys to the future. To draw out the spirit of folk crafts and give it substance within the context of our modern, changing environment is the way to carry on the tradition of Japanese mingei in the present, and to provide direction for the future.

Color Plates

Textiles

Detail of plate 9

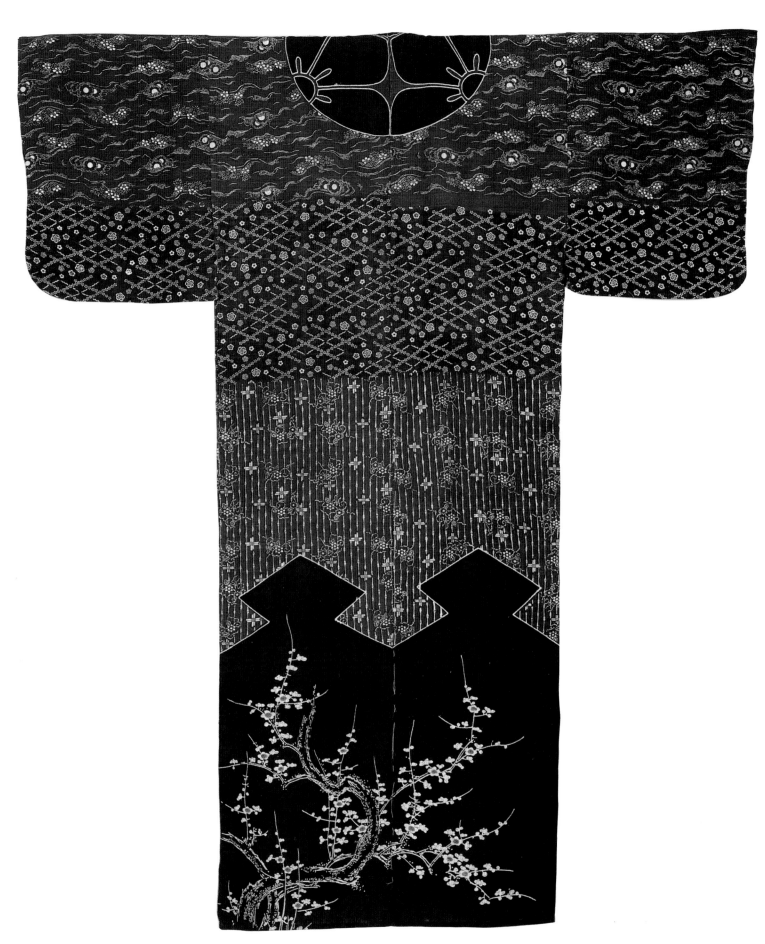

1 Ceremonial hood garment, hemp

36 TEXTILES

2 Ceremonial hood garment, hemp

TEXTILES 37

3, 4 Ceremonial hood garments, hemp

38 TEXTILES

5 Wrapping cloth, cotton

6–8 Kimono-shaped comforters, cotton

40 TEXTILES

TEXTILES 41

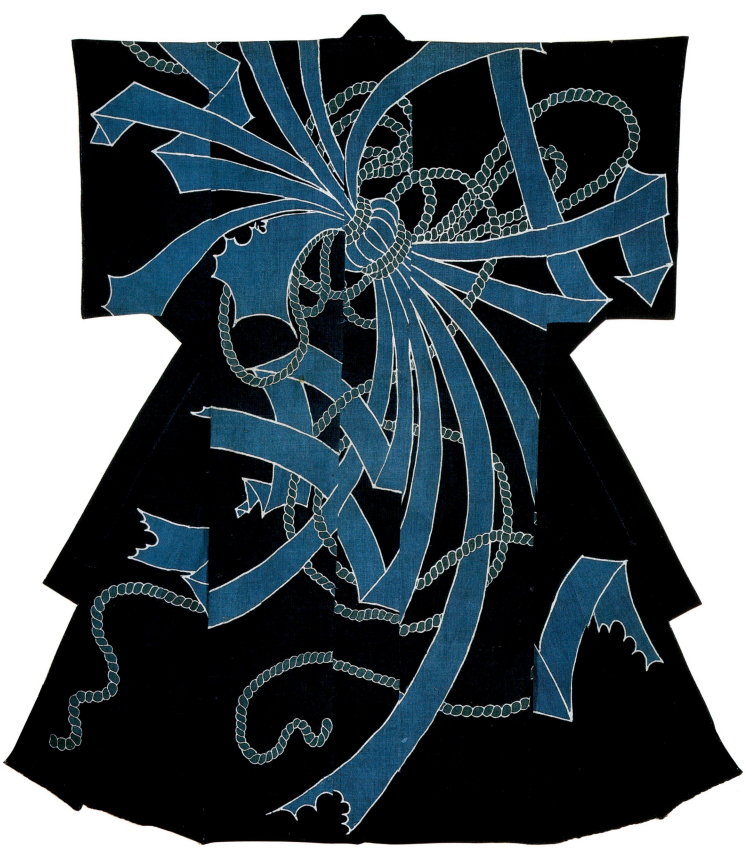

9 Kimono-shaped comforter, cotton

10 Detail of Okinawan kimono, cotton ▶

42 TEXTILES

11 Okinawan kimono, cotton

12 Okinawan kimono, hemp

TEXTILES 45

13 Detail of fireman's coat, deerskin

14

14, 15 Fireman's coat, deerskin

15

TEXTILES 47

16 Bedding cloth, cotton

48 TEXTILES

17 Bedding cloth, cotton

18 Bedding cloth, cotton

19 Bedding cloth, cotton ▶

50 TEXTILES

20 Bedding cloth, cotton (*with detail at left*)

21 Ceremonial covering for horses, cotton

 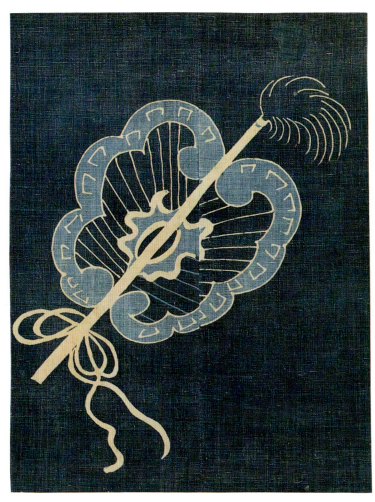

22 Bedding cloth, cotton

TEXTILES

23 Stage curtains with *Eight Views of Ōmi*

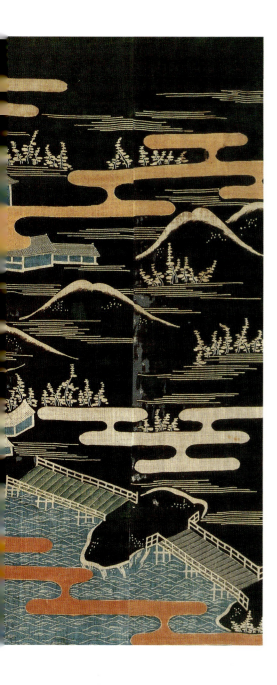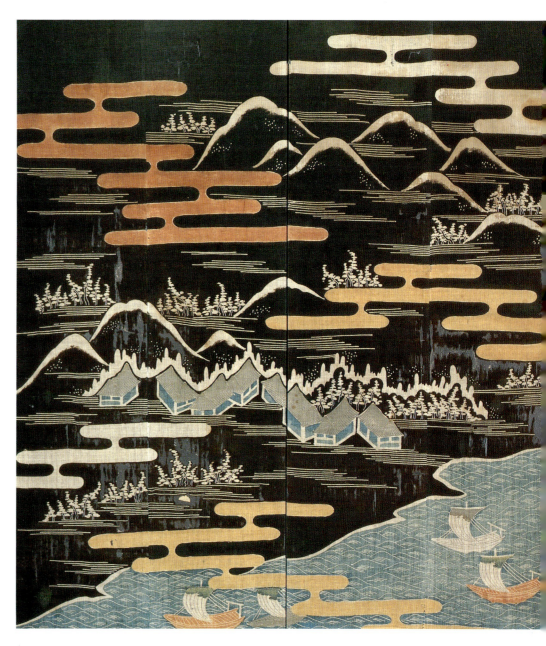

TEXTILES 57

24 Bedding cloth, cotton

25 Cotton cloth

26 Okinawan kimono, cotton

TEXTILES

27

28

27, 28 Details of Okinawan kimono cloth

29 Okinawan cotton cloth

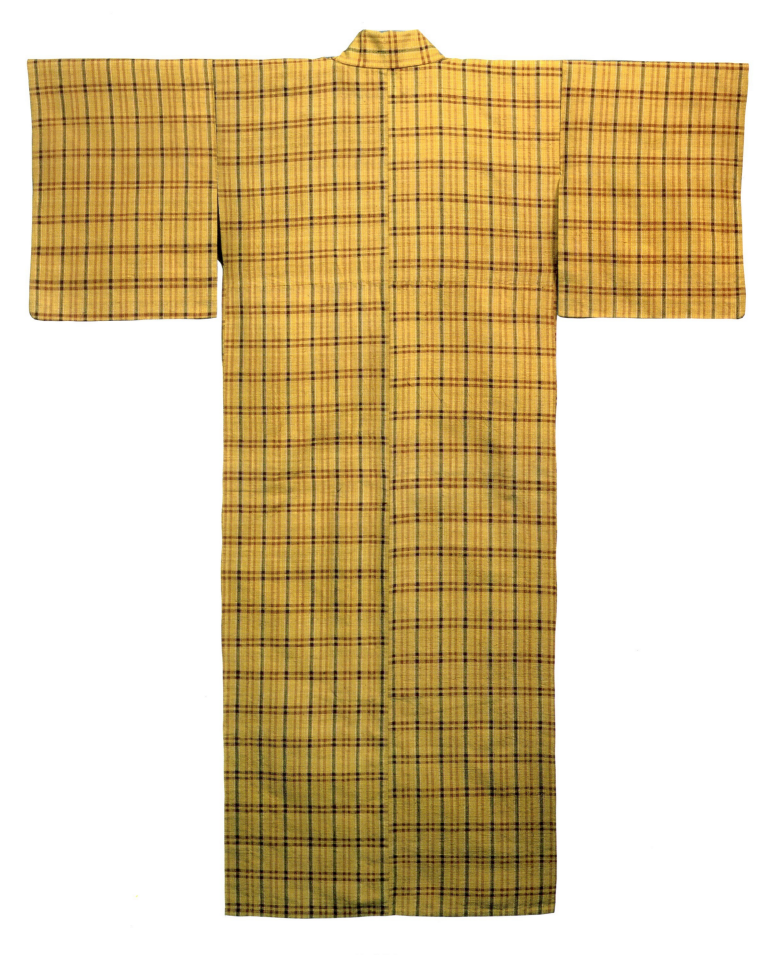

30 Silk kimono

31 Silk kimono

32 Shop curtain, cotton

68 TEXTILES

33 Cotton cloth (*with details at left*)

34 Detail of quilted *sashiko* coat, cotton

35, 36   Quilted *sashiko* coats, cotton

37 Fireman's coat, cotton

72 TEXTILES

38 Quilted *kendō* garment, cotton

39 Ainu robe, elm bark and cotton

40 Ainu robe, cotton

TEXTILES 75

41 Okinawan wrapping cloth, ramie

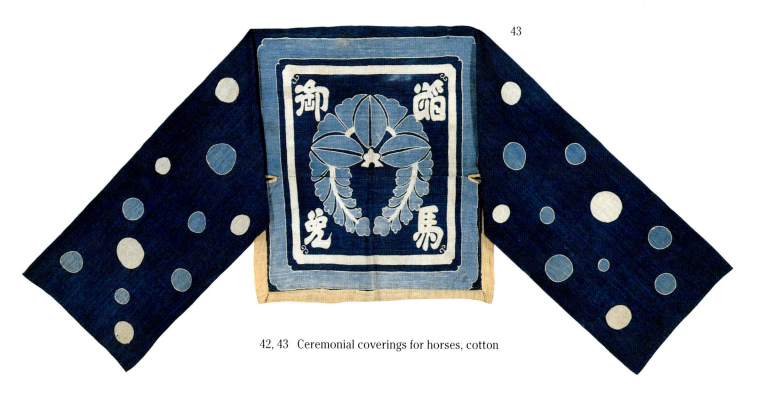

42, 43 Ceremonial coverings for horses, cotton

Ceramics

44   Detail of Tamba stoneware jar

45 Tamba stoneware jar

46 Stoneware jar

CERAMICS 81

47 Okinawan stoneware funerary urn
48 Detail of Okinawan stoneware funerary urn

49–51 Okinawan stoneware votive vases (*left, center*) and Okinawan stoneware saké offering vessel (*right*)

52

53

52, 53 Imari porcelain saké bottles

54 Kutani porcelain dish

55 Karatsu stoneware jar (*with detail at right*)

88 CERAMICS

56 Stoneware bottle

57 Stoneware bottle

58 Imari porcelain bowl

59 Imari porcelain plate

60 Mino stoneware plate (*with detail at left*)

CERAMICS 95

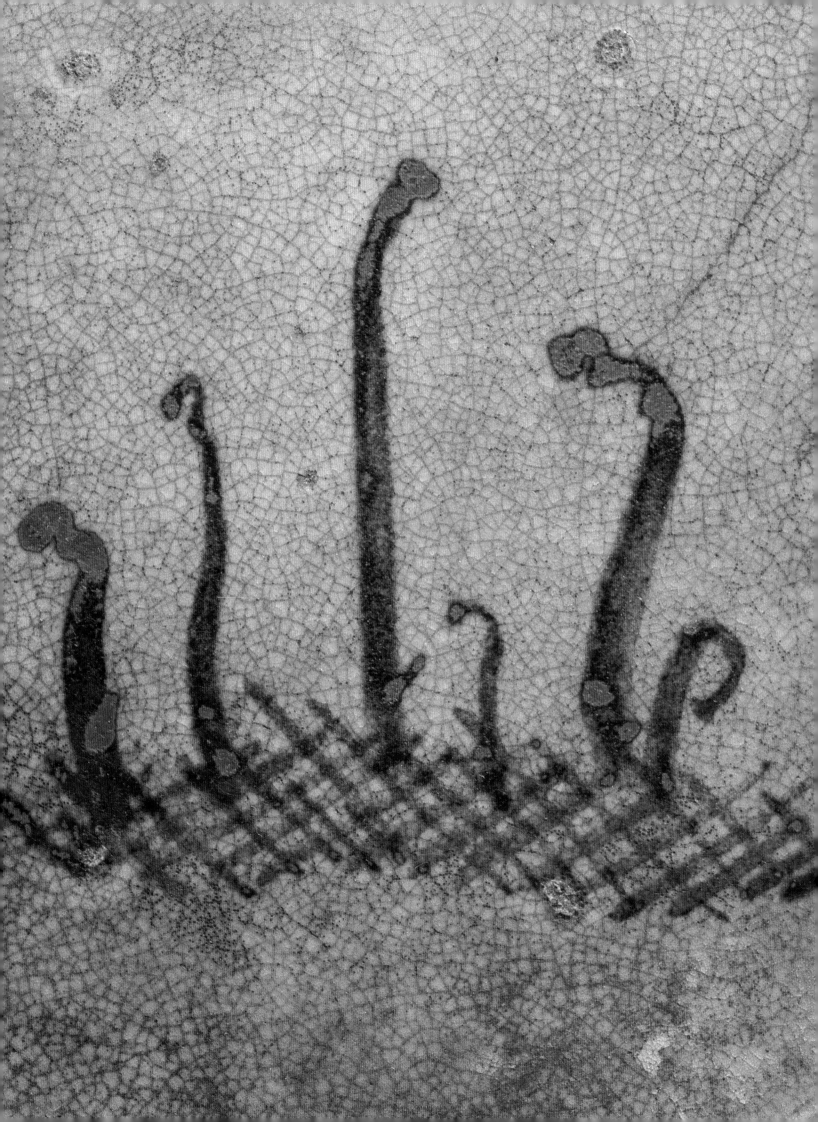

61–63 Seto stoneware oil-drip plates (*with detail of Plate 61 at left*)

CERAMICS 97

64 Imari porcelain jar

65 Imari porcelain oil jar

98 CERAMICS

66 Imari porcelain saké bottle

67 Stoneware bottle

68 Large stoneware saké bottle

69 Stoneware sweet saké jar

70 Stoneware teapot

71–73 Okinawan stoneware saké ewers

74 Okinawan stoneware flower vase

75 Okinawan stoneware saké hip flask

CERAMICS 107

76 Stoneware bowl

77 Stoneware spouted bowl

108 CERAMICS

78 Seto stoneware plate

CERAMICS 109

79 Seto stoneware plate

80 Seto stoneware plate

81, 82 Imari porcelain rice bowls

83, 84 Porcelain teapots/saké pots

CERAMICS 113

85 Imari porcelain bowl

114 CERAMICS

86–88 Imari porcelain bowl and plates

CERAMICS 115

89 Imari porcelain noodle cups and teacups

Modern Ceramics

90

90, 91 Stoneware bowls with white slip

91

92 Stoneware plate with white slip

93 Large Seto stoneware plate

94 Deep stoneware bowl

MODERN CERAMICS 121

95 Large stoneware plate

96 Stoneware spouted bowls

122 MODERN CERAMICS

97, 98 Stoneware saké carafe and teacup

99, 100 Okinawan stoneware bowls

MODERN CERAMICS 123

101

102   101–103 Stoneware teapots

103

104 Stoneware spouted jug

105 Stoneware cooking pot

106 Stoneware lidded bowl

126 MODERN CERAMICS

107 Stoneware plate

Hamada, Kawai, and Leach

108 Stoneware bowl by Shōji Hamada (*with detail at left*)

109, 110 Stoneware flasks by Shōji Hamada

111 Stoneware teacup by Kanjirō Kawai

112 Stoneware plaque by Kanjirō Kawai

113 Slipware plate by Bernard Leach

114 Stoneware plate by Bernard Leach

115, 116 Porcelain plates by Bernard Leach

Wood

117 Detail of chest with metal fittings

118 Lidded box, lacquered wood

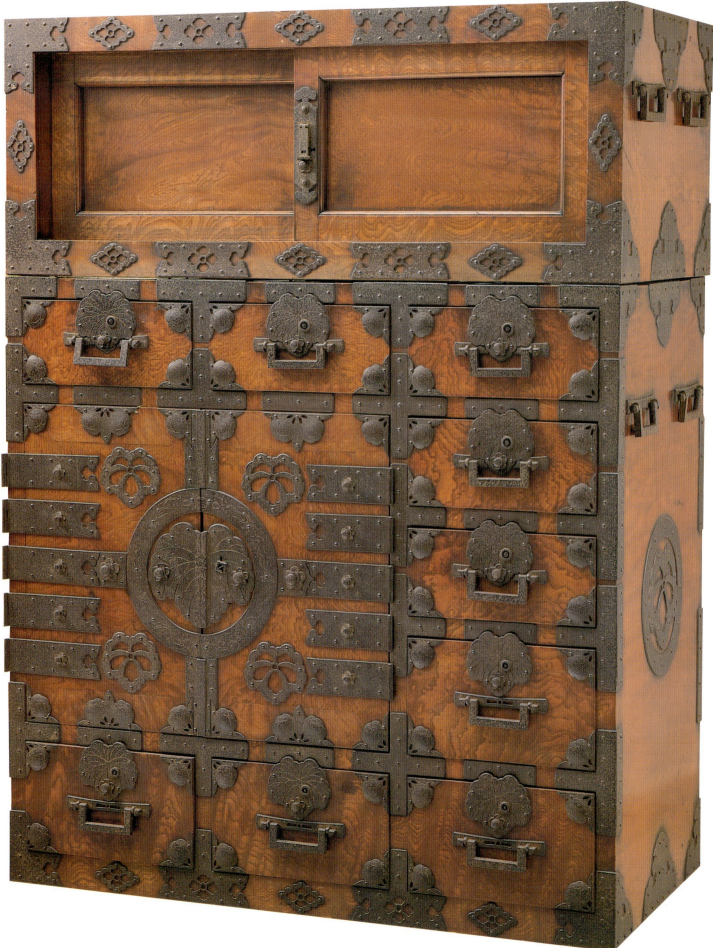

119 Chest, wood with iron fittings

120 Sea chest, wood with iron fittings

121 Pipe holder and tobacco containers, cherry bark

122 Box, cherry bark

WOOD 139

123 Kitchen talisman

124 Lion headdress used in *shishi-mai* dance, lacquered wood

125

125–128 Pot hangers (*bottom*) and crosspieces for suspension (*top*)

126

WOOD 143

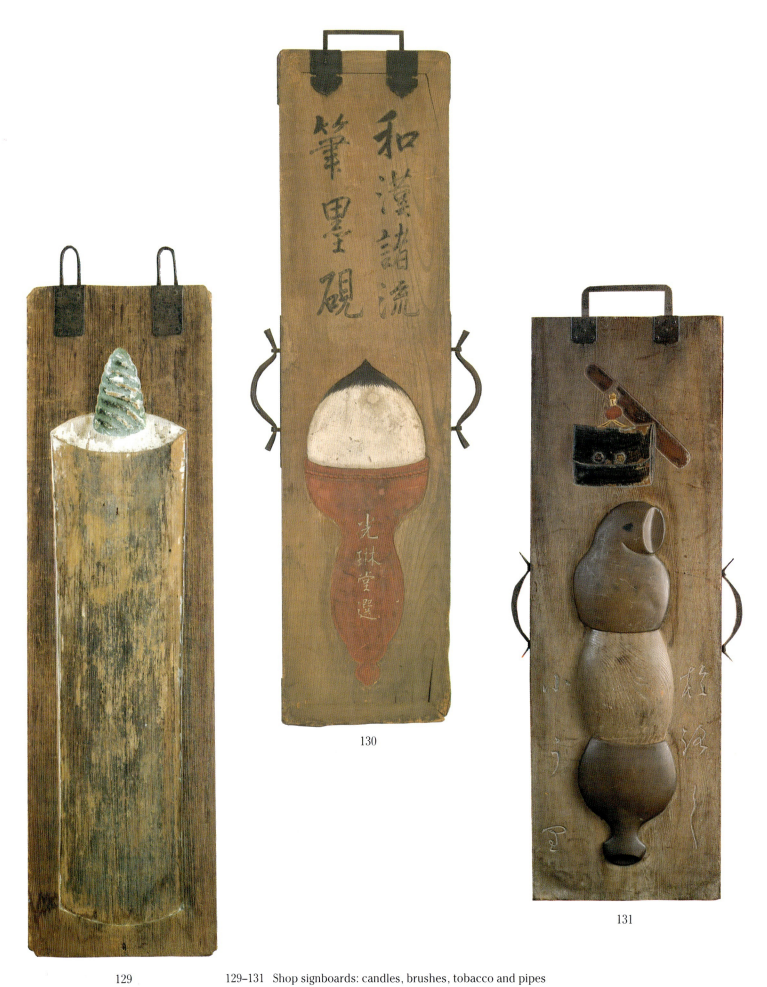

129–131 Shop signboards: candles, brushes, tobacco and pipes

144 WOOD

132 Braided bamboo handbag

133 Straw pannier

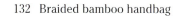

134 Braided bamboo trunk

WOOD 145

Lacquer

135   Detail of lacquer bowl with lid

136

136, 137 Lacquer bowls with gold leaf

137

148 LACQUER

138 Lacquer bowl

139 Lacquer pitcher

LACQUER 149

141 Lacquer spouted bowl

140 Lacquer vase (*with detail at left*)

LACQUER 151

Metal

142 Brass candlestand (*with detail at left*)

143 Brass *hibachi*

144 Brass caldron

145 Brass kettle

146 Iron kettle

Pictorial Art

147 *View of Edo Bay Fortifications*, gouache on paper

148　*View of Western Castle*, gouache on paper

149　*View of Kinokuni Slope*, gouache on paper

150 Rubbing of Buddhist deity, ink on paper

151 Rubbing of roadside folk deities, ink on paper

PICTORIAL ART **161**

152 *Benkei*, ink and color on paper

153 *Monkey, Catfish, and Gourd,* ink and color on paper

154 *Papermaking Village* by Keisuke Serizawa, stencil-dyed cotton

155 *Ryūkyū Scene* by Keisuke Serizawa, stencil-dyed cotton

156 *Straw Cape* by Keisuke Serizawa, stencil-dyed cotton

157 *In Praise of The Tōhoku District* by Shikō Munakata, woodcuts

PICTORIAL ART 167

158 *Goddesses of Heaven and Earth* by Shikō Munakata, ink and color on paper

Notes to the Plates

Much of the information in the Notes to the Plates was adapted by curators of the Japan Folk Crafts Museum from previous writings by Sōetsu Yanagi. In each case, the source is noted at the end of the text. For note on the Frontispiece, Wisteria Maiden, *see note for Plate 152.*

TEXTILES

1 Ceremonial hood garment (*kazuki*). Indigo-dyed hemp with resist designs. 18th century. 151 x 132.5 cm.
2 Ceremonial hood garment (*kazuki*). Indigo-dyed hemp with resist designs. 18th century. 128 x 130 cm.
3 Ceremonial hood garment (*kazuki*). Indigo-dyed hemp with resist designs. 18th century. 130 x 122 cm.
4 Ceremonial hood garment (*kazuki*). Indigo-dyed hemp with resist designs. 155 x 116 cm.

Kazuki are women's garments worn on ceremonial occasions in Fukushima, Yamagata, Akita, and Iwate Prefectures. They are wrapped loosely around the body and draped over the head. Originally, such garments were worn by Kyoto noblewomen, but the custom spread to the distant provinces, where distinctive styles were created. Most are made of hemp, with a large variety of patterns either hand-drawn or dyed with stencils. The patterns are large and exceedingly handsome. (*Kōgei* [Craftwork], No. 84, 1938.)

5 Wrapping cloth (*furoshiki*). Cotton. 19th century. 145 x 120 cm.

This cloth with its bold intersecting pattern of indigo and yellow was dyed by the *nukishime* method. The family crests, skillfully worked into a contrasting arabesque design, are stencil-dyed. Dyehouses used to accept large quantities of orders for such designs.

169

6 Kimono-shaped comforter with family crest and paulownia. Indigo-dyed cotton with resist designs. 19th century. 153 x 156 cm.
7 Kimono-shaped comforter with fan-shaped crest and orange blossoms. Indigo-dyed cotton with resist designs. 19th century. 160 x 155 cm.
8 Kimono-shaped comforter with family crest, pine, and bamboo. Indigo-dyed cotton with resist designs. 19th century. 175 x 145 cm.
9 Kimono-shaped comforter with *noshi* motifs. Indigo-dyed cotton with resist designs. 19th century. 197 x 150 cm.

These represent a type of bedclothes called *yogi*, consisting of cotton cloth that has been stuffed with cotton and sewn into the shape of a kimono. Until the 1940s, *yogi* were commonly used as comforters and draped over sleepers on cold winter nights, but improved indoor heating has made them obsolete. The cloth was dyed using traditional methods, before the onset of the industrial revolution and the introduction of chemical dyes. The designs were hand-drawn by inserting rice paste into a funnel and squeezing it over the fabric before dyeing with indigo, a technique known as *tsutsugaki*. Family crests and auspicious plants and flowers were the most common motifs. The white lines and diverse shades of blue were achieved by varying the frequency of the dye application and resist. The design in Plate 9 is particularly striking, featuring *noshi*—elongated strips of dried abalone used to decorate gifts. Wrapped securely in symbols of good fortune, wearers could drift off to sleep peacefully.

9

6
7
8

10 Okinawan *bingata* kimono. Cotton with stenciled designs. 19th century.
11 Okinawan *bingata* kimono. Cotton with stenciled designs of waves, chrysanthemums, and small birds. 19th century. H. 140 cm.
12 Okinawan *bingata* kimono. Hemp with stenciled designs of chrysanthemums and waves. 19th century. H. 123 cm.

Okinawa is a group of subtropical islands (also known as the Ryūkyū Islands) located at the southernmost end of the Japanese archipelago, on the East China Sea. Its geographical location made it a popular stopping place for trade ships from India and Southeast Asia. Okinawa also had considerable interaction with China from ancient times, and cultural influences from Japan were significant.

Sōetsu Yanagi led an expedition to Okinawa during the latter half of the 1930s to collect textiles, pottery, lacquerware, and other craftwork and to investigate the local language, songs, dances, and drama. Yanagi described Okinawa as a treasure trove of traditional culture and introduced it widely through his magazine devoted to folkcrafts. The Okinawan people were enterprising and creative, but above all they venerated their ancestors and were devoted upholders of tradition. This explains why some aspects of old Japanese culture survive in Okinawa better than in the rest of Japan.

Okinawa became the site of fierce fighting at the close of the Pacific War in 1945 and suffered heavy losses of life along with the destruction of countless cultural artifacts. As a result, the collection of some 1,000 examples of traditional Okinawan craftwork that Yanagi fortuitously acquired for the Japan Folk Crafts Museum now form a priceless record of traditional Okinawan culture. The textiles in particular are astonishingly beautiful.

Okinawan stencil-dyed cloth (*bingata*), with its gorgeous colors and proliferation of nature motifs, is among the most beautiful of all fabrics in the world. The technique of *bingata* is thought to date back to the 15th or 16th century. Indian and Chinese printed cotton fabrics undoubtedly had some influence, but the superior technology and designs of Japanese weavers and dyers contributed more significantly to the brilliant flowering of *bingata*.

Besides dyes and cosmetics imported from southern China, Okinawa dyestuffs include a tall tree called *fukugi* that produces a yellow dye, and a kind of indigo called *karaeno* that grows in the Kunigami district, among others. The beautiful colors of *bingata* are achieved by laboriously applying each hue separately to the cloth by brush; a single kimono may take over a month to finish. The technique of shading known as *kumadori* lends even greater beauty to the stencil-dyed patterns of *bingata*.

which has a history of over 1,000 years, is said to have been transmitted to Japan from India long ago, and it continues to be used today. The characters on the backs of the coats identify the wearers' squads.

13 Fireman's coat. Deerskin with stenciled squad crest design. 19th century. 100 x 140 cm.
14 Fireman's coat. Deerskin with stenciled squad crest design. 19th century. 95 x 130 cm.
15 Fireman's coat. Deerskin with stenciled squad crest design. 19th century. 90 x 133 cm.

These three deerskin coats (*haori*) were formal garments worn by master firefighters in Edo (now Tokyo). The designs were added by applying smoke fumes through a stencil. This stenciling technique,

16 Bedding cloth. Cotton with hand-drawn resist circular floral designs. 19th century. 188 x 235 cm.

These samples of *tsutsugaki*-dyed cloth give a clear impression of the sophisticated skills of early- and mid-19th-century dyers. Flowers of all four seasons are depicted, the essence of each one captured in freely drawn paste-resist designs. Only three basic colors have been used; the beauty of the final product attests to the adroitness of the dyer. Originally intended for bedding, this cloth was later mounted on a screen by Sōetsu Yanagi.

NOTES TO THE PLATES 171

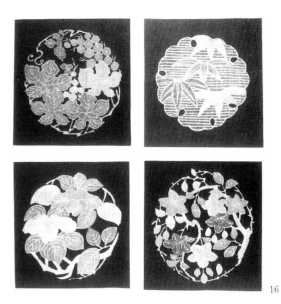

16

18

17 Bedding cloth. Cotton with hand-drawn resist auspicious motifs. 19th century. 155 x 130 cm.

This cloth was dyed using the *tsutsugaki* technique, whereby paste resist was applied to the fabric through a cone. The design consists of five emblems of good fortune: crane and pine, tortoises, bamboo and flowering plum, carp swimming up a waterfall, and peony and Chinese lion. Such auspicious motifs were considered especially appropriate for wedding *futon* (bedding). This example, with its boldly conceived design and masterful resist application, represents the height of Edo-period (1600–1868) dyeing.

19 Bedding cloth. Indigo-dyed cotton with hand-drawn resist designs. 19th century. 128 x 155 cm.

In the early and mid-19th century, flower arrangements and tea ceremony implements were popular motifs for bedding (*futon*), dust covers, and other items in a bride's trousseau. Such designs probably were seen as indications of a woman's level of cultural attainment. Here, the brazier and kettle are placed centrally, surrounded by a charcoal basket at upper right, a mortar on the lower right, and a tea jar on the lower left, as well as a tea whisk, tongs, and other utensils scattered in between.

17

19

20 Bedding cloth. Cotton with hand-drawn resist designs. 19th century. 144 x 95.5 cm.

18 Bedding cloth. Cotton with hand-drawn resist designs.

Symbols of good fortune, long life, and prosperity vary from one culture to another. This cloth is decorated with Japanese auspicious emblems, and skillfully dyed according to the *tsutsugaki* technique. The colors are simple but effective. Now mounted on a screen, this cloth was probably originally used for bedding.

Since paired mandarin ducks are an emblem of connubial bliss and fidelity, this cloth probably was prepared before a wedding by a bride's mother in hopes that the couple might enjoy similar happiness. The sensitive portrayal of the reeds and the birds shows the dyer's high level of skill at using the *tsutsugaki* technique of applying paste resist.

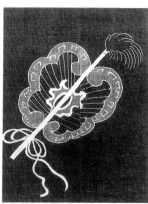

21 Ceremonial covering for horses. Cotton with hand-drawn arabesque and wisteria resist designs. 19th century. 130 x 70 cm.

On festival days, the men who led packhorses carrying freight or passengers would deck out their beloved animals in fancy clothing. Here the family crest of hanging wisteria was produced with a pattern, while the arabesque design was drawn freehand with paste resist. Indigo and vermilion form a bold contrast, and the large design, appropriate for a horse's garment, is well balanced. The garment extended below the horse's loin and was fastened at the saddle.

22 Bedding cloth. Cotton with hand-drawn resist designs. 19th century. 129 x 128 cm.

Fans are associated with good fortune in Japan, and so wedding *futon* (bedding) and other items are often decorated with fan motifs. This fragment is thought to have been part of a larger piece of cloth used for bedding. The design consists of two types of fans, which have been dyed using the *tsutsugaki* technique, in which paste resist is applied to the fabric through a cone. The resist was added in three stages so that three colors—white, light blue, and dark blue—could be skillfully produced using a single dye.

23 Stage curtain with *Eight Views of Ōmi*. Cotton with hand-drawn resist designs. 19th century. 196 x 420 cm.

Following a Chinese precedent, eight famous scenes along the shores of Lake Biwa in Ōmi Province (present-day Shiga Prefecture) were selected for their beauty and called the *Ōmi hakkei*, or *Eight Views of Ōmi*. The scenes, incorporating seasonal references, include Autumn Moon over Ishiyamadera, Sunset Glow over Seta, Clearing Mist at Awazu, Evening Rain at Karasaki, and Descending Geese at Katata. The scenes on this screen were dyed by the *tsutsugaki* method of squeezing paste resist through an applicator directly onto the fabric. Before being made into a screen, this cloth is said to have been a stage curtain at a small theater in the Kinki district (metropolitan Kyoto, Osaka, and Nara; Wakayama, Mie, and Hyōgo Prefectures). The design is splendidly conceived, making effective use of the large space and giving impressive evidence of the masterful skill of mid–Edo-period (1600–1868) dyers in the Kyoto area.

24 Bedding cloth. Indigo-dyed cotton with stenciled designs. 19th century.

These sections of cloth, now mounted on a screen, were all decorated with classic arabesque (*karakusa*) designs used mainly for bedclothes. Cloth with this kind of pattern was produced all over the country, but the stencils used came almost exclusively from a shop called Shirako in Ise, Mie Prefecture. This type of dyed cloth was especially popular in the 19th and early 20th centuries. There was considerable variety in colors as well as designs; the ground could be white, dark blue, or a range of other colors. (*Nihon no Mingei* [Japanese Folkcrafts], 1960.)

NOTES TO THE PLATES 173

24

25 Cloth. Indigo-dyed cotton with pictorial ikat designs. 19th century.

Ikat (*kasuri*) originated in India, passing through Southeast Asia before being transmitted to Japan. The Japanese became fond of weaving pictorial ikat designs, and in the later years of the Edo period (1600–1868), along with increased cultivation of cotton and indigo, ikat fabrics were woven in many parts of the country. The textiles illustrated here (now mounted on a screen) are *e-gasuri* (pictorial ikat) from the San'in district along the Japan Sea coast; they were originally woven as fabric for kimono and bedding. The thread was first indigo-dyed into the desired hues, carefully arranged, and then painstakingly woven. Popular designs included auspicious symbols such as pine, bamboo, and plum, cranes and tortoises, or carp; symbols of power such as tigers and eagles; and other nature motifs as well as ordinary, everyday articles. The rapid rise in machine weaving caused a drop in production, but thanks to the efforts of a small number of people, the technique of traditional *e-gasuri* has been preserved.

25

26 Okinawan kimono. Indigo-dyed cotton with striped ikat pattern. 19th century. 140 x 132 cm.

29 Okinawan kimono cloth. Indigo-dyed cotton with striped ikat pattern. 19th century.

Indigo dyeing, using plants native to the area, flourished in Okinawa. Indigo-dyed cloth like these examples are now used for mounting scrolls, but originally it was woven for kimono. The skillful disposition of stripes and ikat (*kasuri*) has an orderly beauty arising from the mathematical rhythms of the woven cloth.

Okinawa is perhaps best known for its ikat textiles. Nowhere else did *kasuri* achieve the high level of beauty that it did there. The largest designs were reserved for the royal family and nobility, while smaller designs were for the general populace. The former therefore developed mainly in the capital city of Shuri, where the king's castle was located. (*Gekkan Mingei* [Folkcraft Monthly], July 1939.)

27 Okinawan kimono cloth. Ramie with striped ikat pattern. 19th century.

Ramie (*tonbyan*) fiber was introduced to Okinawa from China during the course of long dealings with that country. Textiles woven from this fiber are thin enough to see through, yet strong and resilient, and cool in Okinawa's subtropical climate. The thread was imported, and accordingly expensive, so it was especially popular as a summer garment for the well-to-do. Between the stripes is an ikat (*kasuri*) pattern representing rough water, one of the most common Okinawan designs.

28 Okinawan kimono cloth. Abaca with striped patterns. 19th century.

Indigenous banana plants (*bashō*) produce fine-quality fibers (abaca) that are processed into thread. Such vegetable fibers are tough and resilient, do not stick to the loom, and have high permeability, making them suitable for summer clothing for people living in a sultry, subtropical climate. The techniques of dyeing and weaving banana fiber were transmitted from the south and developed in Okinawa over a long period of time before reaching their final form.

29 See note to Plate 26.

26

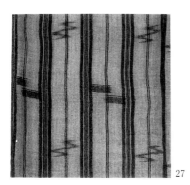

27

28

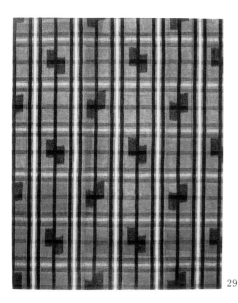

29

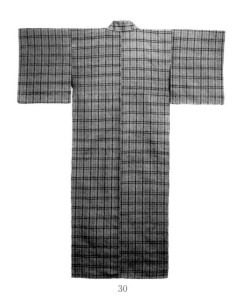

30

30 Kimono. Silk with woven checkerboard design. 20th century. 140 x 134 cm.

This kimono is made of dyed yellow silk known as *kihachijō*. Hachijō weaving began some one hundred years ago on the small island of Hachijōjima. Cloth is woven with silk threads that are taken from local cocoons and dyed with locally made vegetable dyes. Yellow, reddish-yellow, and black predominate. The ability of Hachijō weavers and dyers to create their own distinctive world using only three colors is remarkable.

The dedication of Hachijō artisans offers many lessons about the nature of beauty and true craftsmanship. They use nothing but local materials; they follow a narrow path but develop it to the fullest; they are utterly devoted to their craft; and they never compromise or lower their standards. Hachijō cloth made a century ago is as strong as ever.

31 Kimono. Silk with woven stripes. 19th century. 139 x 138 cm.

The subdued colors and understated beauty of striped kimono fabrics exemplify one aspect of 19th-century Japanese taste. In particular they represent the highly refined aesthetic sensibility that came to be expressed in the word *shibui*. The exact origin of this kimono is not known, but it is thought to be the city of Yūki in central Honshū. Even today Yūki is the home of dedicated craftsmen and -women who take pride in their inherited traditions of weaving and dyeing.

31

32 Shop curtain. Cotton with stenciled designs. 19th century. 160 x 170 cm.

This shop curtain (*noren*) originally hung in front of a Kyoto store. It was printed on the occasion of the opening of a branch family's establishment, using stencils preserved by the main family. The stencil was laid on the cloth, and ink or dye brushed over it. The design of luxuriant bamboo symbolizes prosperity.

NOTES TO THE PLATES 175

33 Cloth. Cotton with stenciled designs. 19th century. 96.5 x 97.5 cm.

This cloth has been decorated with auspicious symbols, including crane, tortoise, and lotus on the upper level; plum blossom, crane, straw coat, and sedge hat on the middle level; and flowing water, chrysanthemum, and shells and water on the bottom level. Each has been arranged in a circular design, the motifs imbued with a flowing sense of movement. The designs were rendered in what seems to be a form of *yūzen* resist dyeing, with the color gradation skillfully done. (*Mingei*, No. 73, 1959.)

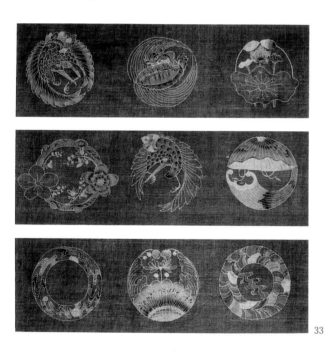

34 Quilted *sashiko* coat. Indigo-dyed cotton. 19th century.
35 Quilted *sashiko* coat. Indigo-dyed cotton. 19th century. 140 x 123 cm.
36 Quilted *sashiko* coat. Indigo-dyed cotton. 19th century. 110 x 132.5 cm.

From the early 19th through the early 20th century, women in the Tsugaru district (western Aomori Prefecture) produced large quantities of quilted garments called *sashiko*, with characteristic white stitching known as *kogin*. At first the stitching was purely utilitarian, done to reinforce and add to the warmth of work clothes, but in time decorative elements prevailed. Tsugaru *kogin* consists of stitching in white cotton thread on cloth dyed a deep shade of indigo. Detailed patterns are stitched in orderly fashion, parallel to the weft, along the top back and across the chest of garments. The simple, geometric designs have the crystalline beauty of snowflakes. As snow piled up outside homes in Japan's northern provinces, wives and daughters passed the long winter days seated at the hearth, learning the art of *kogin* from skilled old women. The intensity of their devotion is revealed in the stitches of these beautiful garments.

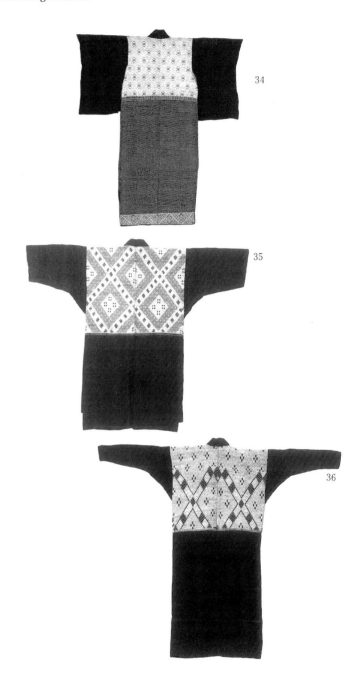

37 Fireman's coat. Indigo-dyed cotton with stitched and hand-drawn resist designs. 19th century. 75 x 135 cm.

This striking *sashiko* garment was worn by a fireman. Reinforced with stitching throughout, it is sturdily made, designed to fit closely and to allow its wearer full freedom of movement. The design on the back, hand-drawn with a paste resist, represents water. In Edo, where Japanese houses built of wood, bamboo, earth, and paper were crowded closely together, fires occurred frequently and the firefighter's job was of utmost importance.

37

39

38 Quilted *kendō* garment. Indigo-dyed cotton. 19th century. 97 x 125 cm.

During the Edo period (1600–1868), samurai were constantly refining their martial skills. It was a time of peace, but every warrior took pride in his swordsmanship. The garment shown here was worn during *kendō*, or fencing practice. An exquisite *sashiko* pattern is stitched on the bright indigo ground. Such work was done painstakingly, over long hours, not by specialized artisans but by the mothers and wives of the wearers.

40

38

41 Okinawan wrapping cloth. Ramie with hand-drawn resist designs. 110 x 114 cm.

In Okinawa, wrapping cloths (*uchakui*) are often dyed by the *tsutsugaki* technique of squeezing paste resist through a tube onto the cloth. (This technique is known as *nuihichi* in Okinawa.) Wrapping cloths range in size from large (180 cm) to small (30 cm). Most are made of ramie or hemp, but some are made of cotton or, more rarely, silk. Circular designs with pine, bamboo, plum blossom, chrysanthemum, peony, iris, or other flowers are common. Sometimes a family crest, or an auspicious symbol such as crane or tortoise, is added.

39 Ainu robe. Elm bark and cotton with embroidery and appliqué. 19th century. 118 x 130 cm.
40 Ainu robe. Cotton with embroidery and appliqué. 19th century. 127 x 124 cm.

The Ainu, an indigenous people living in the northern extremity of the Japanese archipelago, possess a language and culture distinct from those of the rest of Japan. Today a small number of Ainu in Hokkaido carry on the ancestral traditions, preserving the unique heritage of their language and folk customs.

Of the costumes shown here, Plate 39 is woven from the inner bark fibers of elm trees, while Plate 40 is made of cotton obtained from the Japanese. They are each decorated with embroidery and appliqué along the collar, sleeves, back, and hem. The designs are talismanic, traditionally believed by the Ainu to have magical properties to ward off evil influences.

41

42, 43 Ceremonial coverings for horses. Indigo-dyed cotton. 19th century.

Until modern forms of transportation were introduced, horses were indispensable to daily life in Japan, serving as steeds for warriors, legs for travelers and peddlers, and agricultural tools for farmers. People took pride in their horses and treated them with loving care. For celebrations and other special days, they would dress their favorite horses in special garments. The two horse coverings illustrated here were dyed with indigo using two techniques: *tsutsugaki*, wherein the design is hand-drawn with a paste resist, and *katazome*, dyeing with a stencil. The writing on Plate 43 says "Horse going by, be careful." The part of Plate 42 where the saddle would sit bears a hand-drawn family crest; the geometric pattern below it—repeating hexagons—is stencil-dyed.

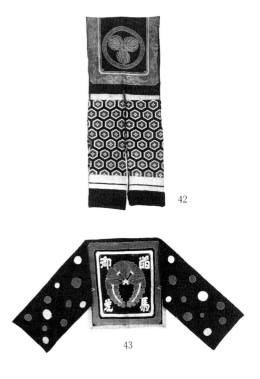

CERAMICS

44 Large jar. Tamba stoneware, natural ash glaze. Muromachi period (1333–1568). H. 41.5 cm.

Kilns producing Tamba ware in present-day Hyōgo Prefecture are said to date back to the early Kamakura period (1185–1333). During the Momoyama period (1568–1600), with the rise of the tea ceremony, Tamba potters came to fire tea bowls and other tea implements. However, most Tamba pottery consists of bowls, jars, bottles, and ewers suited to the daily needs of the local farming population. These wares were fired in *noborigama*—climbing kilns constructed on mountain slopes.

Tamba kilns are fueled by Japanese red pine taken from the surrounding hills; falling wood ash sifts down upon pottery inside the kiln, melting in the high temperature and adhering to the surfaces. The resulting greenish glaze thus occurs accidentally. Early practitioners of the tea ceremony were attracted to the subdued beauty of such natural glazes, as was Sōetsu Yanagi. Among the large number of Tamba ceramics he collected, this jar stands out as a particularly fine example showing the beauty of natural glaze.

45 Jar. Tamba stoneware, iron glaze with natural ash deposits. 18th century. H. 42 cm.

This jar was produced in Tachikui, Tamba, in Hyōgo Prefecture. The handles suggest that it may have held tea leaves. Iron glaze has been splashed on, trailing to form a decorative design. During firing, ashes from the wood-burning kiln also fused with the clay to form patches of natural glaze.

46 Storage jar. Yumino stoneware, iron glaze over white slip. Late 18th century. H. 25 cm.

Jars like this have recently begun passing into the hands of collectors, but it was not long ago that they lived in the murky light of country kitchens. Produced at Yumino near Arita in Kyushu, Yumino ceramics share certain features with Karatsu stoneware. Yumino ware is especially famous for its bold designs; here the pine motif is so abbreviated that it is almost unrecognizable, but the animated brushwork imbues the jar with a vivacious sense of freedom. (*Kōgei* [Craftwork], No. 22, 1932.)

46

47 Okinawan funerary urn. Stoneware. 20th century. H. 50 cm.
48 Okinawan funerary urn. Stoneware. 20th century.

The Okinawan word *jiishii* is a variant of *zushi*, a miniature shrine in a temple; these funerary urns are called *jiishigame*. In Okinawa it is customary to wash the bones of the dead and place them in these repositories, which are accordingly large and spacious. Urns containing the bones of an entire clan are set on raised platforms inside one huge grave. The most ancient urns are made of wood or stone. Later they came to be made of unglazed pottery, then, gradually, of glazed pottery. Both glazed and unglazed varieties continue to be made, the latter generally on a potter's wheel, the former from molds.

Jiishiigame are decorated with special designs, of which the most common is the lotus motif. There are a variety of other designs, including Buddhist images in relief, demon masks, and killer whales. All the urns have lids, which are more elaborate than the bodies. Excessive decoration can signal the decline of a tradition, but here the effect remains powerful, perhaps because faith in the spirits of the dead remains a vital force. Typical glaze colors are green, amber, and blue. (*Kōgei* [Craftwork], No. 103, 1940.)

47

48

49 Okinawan votive vase. Stoneware, white slip and amber glaze. 19th century. H. 17.1 cm.
50 Okinawan votive vase. Stoneware, white slip and cobalt blue glaze. 19th century. H. 17.2 cm.
51 Okinawan saké offering vessel. Stoneware, white slip and amber glaze. 19th century. H. 19.3 cm.

The central and left-hand ceramics are vases used on household Buddhist altars. At the right is a container used for offerings of saké. All three are products of Tsuboya in Okinawa. Over a white slip ground, lines, dots, and lotus blossoms have been incised using a nail or some such instrument, and then a cobalt (*gosu*) or honey glaze has been applied.

49   50   51

52 Saké bottle. Imari porcelain, underglaze cobalt blue. 18th century. H. 13.8 cm.
53 Saké bottle. Imari porcelain, underglaze cobalt blue. 18th century. H. 14 cm.

These small saké bottles (*tokkuri*) were made to be set on a household altar as offerings to the gods. The one on the right has a dense scroll pattern resembling the tightly curled arms of an octopus, while the one on the left has a simple linear design.

NOTES TO THE PLATES   179

54 Dish. Kutani porcelain, overglaze enamels. 17th century. D. 36.4 cm.

Kutani porcelain, which developed in the first half of the 17th century as a ware for the powerful Maeda daimyo in what is now Ishikawa Prefecture, is considered with Imari ware to be one of Japan's finest overglaze enamel wares. The techniques of producing overglaze enamels are said to have been introduced to Japan by immigrant Chinese potters fleeing from Ming China (1368–1644). However, the efforts of Japanese potters gave birth to a distinctly different world of beauty. This dish, with its design of kingfisher and lotus, is a superb example of the golden period of Old Kutani ware.

56 Spouted bottle. Stoneware, iron glaze with white and yellow overglaze. 19th century. H. 20 cm.

This pouring vessel, known as an *unsuke*, is a kitchen utensil used to hold saké, vinegar, or soy sauce. It was made in the village of Koishihara, Fukuoka Prefecture, Kyushu. White and yellow overglaze have been splashed over an iron glaze. The pleasantly rustic air of this bottle is typical of folk wares.

57 Spouted bottle. Stoneware, iron glaze with green drip overglaze. 19th century. H. 28 cm.

This bottle (*unsuke*) is the product of a kiln in the Nishishinmachi district of Fukuoka City, Kyushu. The area flourished after potters from the village of Koishihara moved here early in the 18th century and produced a wide variety of wares for the local daimyo as well as the populace. During the Meiji period (1868–1911), however, Nishishinmachi gradually was abandoned until a single kiln site is all that remains. The bottle shown here is of a type used in commoner kitchens up to the beginning of the Shōwa period (1926–89).

55 Jar. Karatsu stoneware, underglaze iron. 16th century. H. 14 cm.

The Karatsu kilns in Kita Kyushu were founded by Korean potters brought back to Japan by warriors involved in the Korea campaigns at the end of the 16th century. Not surprisingly, Karatsu ware bears a great resemblance to Korean Yi dynasty ceramics. This jar was thought to be a *mizusashi*, a vessel for holding fresh water during the tea ceremony, until Sōetsu Yanagi established that it was made originally as a kitchen saltcellar. Designed primarily to be useful, this jar demonstrates the natural beauty of objects fired by anonymous potters not consciously seeking to create works of art.

58 Bowl. Imari porcelain, underglaze cobalt blue. 17th century. D. 47.5 cm.

Imari porcelain was first made in the late Momoyama period (1568–1600) by the naturalized Korean potter Ri Sampei (1579–1655), who was brought to Japan in 1598. Ri Sampei found clay for porcelain production in the Arita area of Kyushu and fired the first plain white, as well as the first underglaze blue, porcelains in Japan. From then on Arita developed until the area grew to rival Ching-te Chen in China as a production center of fine porcelain.

When Japan entered its long period of national seclusion in the 17th century, Dutch traders in Nagasaki helped to disseminate Arita ware overseas as far as Europe. Since Imari Harbor served as the port from which Arita ware was shipped, the name "Imari" was applied to all white, underglaze blue, and red enameled porcelain wares from Arita. The bowl shown here is representative of the fine quality of Imari underglaze blue. It has a sleek finish and the landscape has been masterfully painted.

58

59 Plate. Imari porcelain, underglaze cobalt blue with overglaze enamels. 17th century. D. 44 cm.

The decoration on this fine large Imari plate, fired in Arita, is suggestive of a *yūzen*-dyed kimono. In the center is a traditional design, influenced by Chinese porcelain, of a garden fence surrounded by flowers; various *yūzen* motifs are scattered around the edge of the plate. Brightly colored overglaze enameled porcelain wares such as this were popular not only in Japan but in Europe, where they won admiration and sparked interest in Asia.

59

60 Plate. Mino stoneware. Late 16th century. D. 24.5 cm.

The Mino area (present-day Gifu Prefecture) has kilns dating back to the Heian period (794–1185). This shallow plate was originally used as tableware. The glaze melted during firing to form a beautiful white finish. The design of ripe millet was casually drawn in underglaze iron, with the abbreviated style and masterful control born of long practice. A fine example of painted Momoyama period (1568–1600) pottery, this plate is one of the treasures of the Japan Folk Crafts Museum's ceramics collection.

60

61 Oil-drip plate. Stoneware, underglaze iron. 19th century. D. 19 cm.
62 Oil-drip plate. Stoneware, underglaze iron. 19th century. D. 22 cm.
63 Oil-drip plate. Stoneware, underglaze iron. 19th century. D. 23 cm.

Plates like these were used to contain oil for lanterns (*andon*) and placed under them to catch the drippings. Until sixty or seventy years ago, they were fired in large quantities in Seto kilns, especially in Shinano. Most have underglaze iron paintings, and a fair number have patches of green glaze. Production began to decline in the early Meiji period (1868–1911), and finally such plates were completely replaced by brass ones. For a time, however, they were widely used in private homes in the countryside, especially in Aichi, Kagawa, Mie, and Shiga Prefectures, as well as in Kyoto. ("Kōgei no Michi" [The Way of Crafts], 1928.)

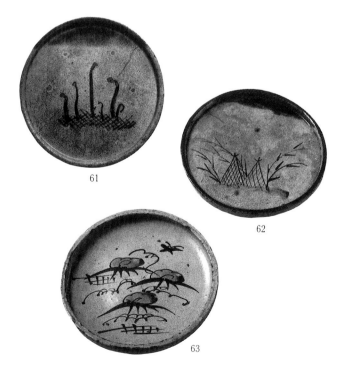
61 62 63

64 Jar. Imari porcelain, underglaze cobalt blue. 17th century. H. 13 cm.

Imari porcelain utensils often bear fishnet patterns, a design that probably originated in China. It is somewhat unusual for a jar of this shape to be decorated with fishnet patterns, but here the design and vessel complement one another beautifully. (*Mingei Zukan* [Encyclopedia of Folkcrafts], 1960.)

65 Oil jar. Imari porcelain, overglaze enamels. 18th century. H. 9.2 cm.

In the Edo period (1600–1868), women's hairstyles became extremely varied and artistic; women took equal pains with their hair and makeup. This charming Imari porcelain bottle was a container for scented hair oil. The design of a peony in full bloom is skillfully executed with the sure, simple brushstrokes of someone who painted the same motif over and over again.

66 Saké bottle. Imari porcelain, underglaze cobalt blue. 18th century. H. 23.5 cm.

This type of saké bottle must have been especially popular, for a great many survive. Such utensils were produced swiftly and casually in large numbers. The fishnet decoration is well-suited to the shape of the bottle, illustrating the inseparability of design and form. The fine lines of the design are particularly admirable. (*Mingei Zukan* [Encyclopedia of Folkcrafts], 1960.)

67 Bottle. Kumamoto stoneware, white overglaze with engraved designs. 19th century. H. 32 cm.

The Shōdai kiln, founded by Korean potters, is one of the oldest in Kumamoto Prefecture. For three centuries it has continued to produce miscellaneous household wares, as well as tea ceremony utensils. A fine example is this bottle, with its large leaf design scratched by nail in the dripped-on white overglaze.

68 Large saké bottle. Saga stoneware, white slip with combed and finger-painted designs. 18th century. H. 32.5 cm.

The technique used to decorate this saké bottle originated in Hizen, Saga Prefecture. First a white slip was brushed over the surface from the neck to the lower part of the bottle; then designs were combed and finger-painted, exposing the dark clay beneath. Finally a green or honey glaze was splashed over the entire vessel.

69 Sweet saké jar. Naeshirogawa stoneware, iron glaze. 19th century. H. 28 cm.

This is an example of *kuromon*, or blackware, of the Naeshirogawa region of Kagoshima Prefecture. Designs of chrysanthemums, peonies, and other plants are common. The iron glaze was applied thickly to achieve an effect like black lacquer. The shape is compact, and overall the piece has a distinctively Japanese air and a depth of character that ensure it a lasting place as a representative work of folk art. (*Mingei Zukan* [Encyclopedia of Folkcrafts], 1960.)

69

70 Teapot. Stoneware. 20th century. H. 17 cm.

This teapot was made in the town of Mashiko, Tochigi Prefecture, and typifies the type of ware produced there from the early 19th century to the present. Painted with a minimal number of brushstrokes, the simplified landscape decoration was perfected over the years by craftsmen producing large numbers of such wares.

71 Okinawan saké ewer. Stoneware, white and cobalt blue glaze. 19th century. H. 9.9 cm.
72 Okinawan saké ewer. Stoneware, white and cobalt blue glaze. 19th century. H. 9 cm.
73 Okinawan saké ewer. Stoneware, white glaze. 19th century. H. 9.6 cm.

This type of saké pouring vessel is called a *chūka* in Okinawa. The origin of the word is thought to be *shuke*, or saké house. *Chūka* were made in a wide range of styles, with designs incised, brushed, or dotted, and with glazes of bright blue or white. The rich variety is ample evidence of the pride and pleasure Okinawans take in their fine local saké, *awamori*.

74 Okinawan flower vase. Stoneware, underglaze cobalt blue. H. 29.5 cm.

This receptacle was designed for offering flowers to the souls of the deceased. Two kinds were produced: wide-mouthed vases in traditional Japanese style and cylindrical ones like this. The bamboo painting on this vase was rendered in a free and simple style with enormous appeal. (*Kōgei* [Craftwork], No. 99, 1939.)

75 Okinawan saké hip flask. Stoneware, iron glaze. 20th century. H. 19.4 cm.

This type of crescent-shaped, portable saké container is known colloquially as a *dachibin*. It would have been fastened to a string around the waist, so as to be handy for journeys or for festivals. *Dachibin* have ceased to be made, but at one time kilns turned out large quantities. They were decorated in a variety of ways: applied black or colored glazes, elaborate inlaid designs, relief designs, or dripped glazes. (*Kōgei* [Craftwork], No. 99, 1939.)

76 Large bowl. Tatenoshita stoneware, *namako* glaze. 20th century. D. 31 cm.

Many miscellaneous everyday wares like this bowl were fired from the beginning of the 19th century until the Shōwa period (1926–89) at the Tatenoshita kiln, in Nakamura, Soma City, Fukushima Prefecture. Large urns and bowls were especially common. The gray glaze on this heavy, massive bowl is known as *namako*.

76

77 Large spouted bowl. Nagaoka stoneware, *namako* glaze. 20th century. D. 43 cm.

The Nagaoka kiln in the village of Minamitono, still active today, is the largest folk kiln in Akita Prefecture. The products of this kiln are extremely free, strong, and a bit wild. They include urns, large bowls, jars, bottles, and spouted bowls. All are covered with *namako* glaze. (*Genzai no Nihon Minyō* [Contemporary Japanese Folk Kilns], 1942.)

77

78 Plate. Seto stoneware, underglaze iron "horse eye" design. 19th century. D. 33 cm.
79 Plate. Seto stoneware, underglaze cobalt and iron crane design. 19th century. D. 34.5 cm.
80 Plate. Seto stoneware, underglaze cobalt and iron landscape design. 19th century. D. 36 cm.

These are serving plates, subject to hard use in the kitchen; the rich variety of pictorial designs they bear are eloquent testimony to the lively skills of artisans specializing in such decoration. While these examples are all large, plates were made in three sizes—large, medium, and small. It was customary to attach a wide rim. The painted designs were brushed rapidly, in an offhand yet confident manner. Landscapes such as the one in Plate 80 are extremely rare. The kind of plate exemplified by Plate 78, with its spiral "horse-eye" design brushed in underglaze iron, was popular in inns and eating places along the Tōkaidō Road. (*Mingei Zukan* [Encyclopedia of Folkcrafts], 1960.)

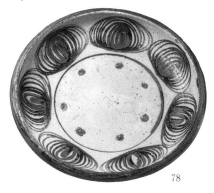
78

79

80

81 Rice bowl. Imari porcelain, underglaze cobalt blue. 18th century. H. 9 cm.
82 Rice bowl. Imari porcelain, underglaze cobalt blue. 18th century. H. 8.5 cm.

Lidded bowls such as these represent another important type of Imari ware. They served many purposes and exhibit a great deal of variety in both form and design. The lids kept the rice from getting cold, and when removed and set on the table, they also served as handy small plates. The design of the left-hand bowl is of unusual excellence. No modern rice bowl can compare with it. The spiral resembling a signature appearing on the lid of the right-hand bowl was probably added by a supervisor to keep track of the number of works produced by an individual potter or kiln. (*Mingei Zukan* [Encyclopedia of Folkcrafts], 1960.)

83 Teapot/Saké pot. Hirasa porcelain, underglaze cobalt blue. 18th century. H. 8.8 cm.
84 Teapot/Saké pot. Imari porcelain, underglaze cobalt blue. 18th century. H. 20 cm.

The vessel in Plate 83 was used in Okinawa not for tea, but for rare old *awamori*, or saké. It was probably ordered from Satsuma in Kyushu. Plate 84 was also used as a saké container at weddings or other festive occasions. Its handle incorporates a plethora of auspicious motifs. The designs on both vessels were rendered with cobalt glaze on a white ground. (*Shokoku no Dobin* [Teapots from Around Japan], 1943.)

85 Bowl. Imari porcelain, underglaze cobalt blue. 18th century. D. 25.5 cm.

Scattered on the inner and outer surfaces of this bowl are roundels with dragons, jewels, sedge hats, and scrolls drawn using a type of liquid cobalt. The dragons seem friendly rather than formidable, giving the bowl a disarming cheerfulness. Chinese-influenced designs take on a distinctly Japanese charm when rendered in such a relaxed manner.

86 Bowl. Imari porcelain, underglaze cobalt blue design of pine, bamboo, and plum blossoms.

Bowls of this sort survive today in very large numbers. Designs of plum blossoms are particularly common, many executed with great freedom and verve. This bowl is a typical example; the fact that its design was painted on great quantities of wares in no way diminishes its appeal. (*Mingei Zukan* [Encyclopedia of Folkcrafts], 1960.)

87 Plate. Imari porcelain, underglaze cobalt blue. 18th century. D. 17.5 cm.

A cherry blossom design is repeated three times around the edge of this plate. It is simple, but the drawing is incomparably beautiful, the brushwork free. The cobalt blue has a high iron content, so the color is somewhat muddy; this gives the work a quiet appeal, reminding us of the beauty inherent in natural materials. (*Mingei Zukan* [Encyclopedia of Folkcrafts], 1960.)

88 Plate. Imari porcelain, underglaze cobalt blue. 18th century. D. 17.5 cm.

This plate is an example of the ware popularly known as *kurawanka* ("won't you eat?"), which survives in great quantities. There is a correspondingly large number of designs, many of which have extraordinary charm. This plate is a good example; the design skillfully interweaves fans and what appear to be fish baskets, and the coloring is beautifully done. (*Mingei Zukan* [Encyclopedia of Folkcrafts], 1960.)

89 a, b, c, d, f, g: Noodle cups. Imari porcelain, underglaze cobalt blue.
  a. 18th century. H. 5 cm.
  b. 18th century. H. 5.3 cm.
  c. 18th century. H. 6.1 cm.
  d. 17th century.
  f. 18th century. H. 5 cm.
  g. 18th century. H. 5.5 cm.

Sōetsu Yanagi discussed these cups in his book *Ai-e no choku*:

> Works like these are what first drew me to the beauty of common utensils. My collection got its start with these very cups. The variety of motifs painted on them awakened me to the wonders of the world of design; from them I also learned the beauty of underglaze blue. Of all the porcelain with cobalt blue paintings in Japan, those of Imari ware are the most beautiful, as these cups demonstrate. . . . Few wares were as appreciated as these, because they could be used in so many different ways. As the common term *soba choku* indicates, they were frequently used to hold broth for noodle dishes of *soba* or *udon*. At other times they were used for tea or water. Serious saké drinkers, of whom rural Japan has its full share, liked them for their extra capacity. These cups also were used as *mukōzuke*, serving utensils for sashimi and vinegared foods. They could change their role freely as needed. Probably no other vessel was as handy.

The white ground of these porcelain cups is flawless, and the underglaze cobalt decoration has a restrained beauty. The designs show a great freedom and creativity, painted with superlative brushwork that is the product of long years of practice. Beautiful to look at and pleasant to touch, these cups are even more agreeable to use. (*Mingei Zukan* [Encyclopedia of Folkcrafts], 1960.)

89 e, h: Teacups. Imari porcelain, underglaze cobalt blue. 18th century.
  e: H. 5.1 cm.
  h: H. 5.2 cm.

These teacups, known colloquially as *kurawanka* ("won't you drink?"), were fired in large numbers during the Edo period (1600–1868) at folk kilns in Hizen (present-day Nagasaki Prefecture). Using no other color but cobalt blue, craftsmen created an endless variety of designs. Besides scenery, grasses, trees, and flowers, motifs included birds and animals, insects and fish, and almost every other conceivable object. Local, easily available clays were used to create these strangely powerful wares. Had local materials been spurned in favor of fine-quality, pure-white porcelain clay, this special flavor would have been lost. (*Mingei* [Folkcraft], No. 73, 1959.)

89

91

101

92

102

103

104

Contemporary Ceramics

90 Bowl. Stoneware, white slip with brushed designs. 20th century. D. 27 cm.
91 Bowl. Stoneware, white slip with combed designs. 20th century. D. 26.5 cm.
92 Large plate. Stoneware, white slip with brushed designs. 20th century. D. 53 cm.
101–103 Teapots. Stoneware. 20th century. H. 16 cm each.
104 Spouted jug. Stoneware, amber glaze with green splash overglaze. 20th century. H. 46.5 cm.

These ceramics (with the exception of Plate 101) were all produced at the Onta kiln, located in the hamlet of Onta Sarayama near the city of Hita in Ōita Prefecture, Kyushu. Even today potters continue to carry on traditional techniques and customs such as the use of *karausu* (Chinese pestles) to crush the hard local clay. The kiln produces everyday wares of an extraordinary diversity. Onta ware is particularly known for its splash overglazes of amber or green (Plates 102–104) and the use of white slip with brushed (Plates 90, 92) or combed (Plate 91) designs. (*Shokoku no Dobin* [Teapots from Around Japan], 1943.)

93 Large plate. Seto stoneware. 20th century. D. 47.5 cm.

The city of Seto in Aichi Prefecture is one of the oldest centers of ceramic production in Japan. Among the many kilns there, the Hongyō kiln still fires everyday utensils such as plates, bowls, and teacups using traditional methods. Here an interesting design has been created by applying glazes of three different colors.

90

93

94 Deep bowl. Aizu Hongō stoneware, white glaze with green drip overglaze. 20th century. D. 35.5 cm.

The Aizu Hongō kiln in Fukushima Prefecture is representative of ceramic production in the Tōhoku region. The everyday utensils made here include rectangular containers, covered vessels, and deep bowls, like this one. Green glaze was dripped over the initial coating of white glaze.

95 Large plate. Ushinoto stoneware, black and green glaze. 20th century. D. 9.5 cm.
96 Spouted bowls. Ushinoto stoneware, black and green glaze. 20th century. Large bowl: D. 18.5 cm. Left: D. 15 cm. Right: D. 12 cm.

These utensils with lustrous black and green glazes are from the Ushinoto kiln in Tottori Prefecture. This glazing technique is often found in old Seto wares, but at Ushinoto it represents a new approach. The local clay is very hard, almost like porcelain, so the wares are strong. (*Genzai no Nihon Minyō* [Contemporary Japanese Folk Kilns], 1942.)

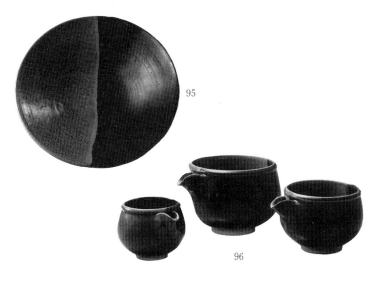

97 Teacup. Ryūmonji stoneware. 20th century. H. 5 cm.
98 Saké carafe. Ryūmonji stoneware. 20th century. H. 14.5 cm.

The Ryūmonji kiln in Kagoshima Prefecture is one of the most important folk kilns in Kyushu. Historically, and even today, this kiln has produced highly distinctive wares of a sort found nowhere else, often with equally distinctive names. This type of saké holder is called a *karakara*, a name that is also used in Okinawa. Ryūmonji utensils are always decorated with a green and honey glaze on a white ground, reminiscent of the famous T'ang dynasty three-color wares. (*Genzai no Nihon Minyō* [Contemporary Japanese Folk Kilns], 1942.)

99 Okinawan bowl. Yomitan stoneware, white slip with overglaze. 20th century. D. 25.5 cm.
100 Okinawan bowl. Yomitan stoneware, white slip with overglaze. 20th century. D. 24.5 cm.

These ceramics are products of the Yomitan kiln in Zakimi, Okinawa Prefecture, where the traditional method of firing in a climbing kiln (*noborigama*) is still carried on with great vigor. Such bowls, known as *wanpū*, are indispensable for Okinawan food, and are made in a variety of shapes and sizes. These two bowls, with designs in cobalt and two-colored (green and amber) glazes over a white slip, overflow with a robust sense of life.

101–104 See note to Plate 90.

105 Cooking pot. Saga stoneware. 20th century. D. 25 cm.

This pot was used to make rice gruel and thus placed directly over a fire. While it has a fragile appearance, it is actually quite strong. It exemplifies the kind of folk utensils produced from the early 17th century up to the present day in Shiraishi, Saga Prefecture.

NOTES TO THE PLATES

106 Lidded bowl. Shinano stoneware, white slip over dark ground. 20th century. D. 25 cm.

This bowl is a product of a kiln located in Shinano, one of many kilns in the Seto area of Aichi Prefecture. Various everyday utensils are fired there. This distinctive lidded pot with white slip applied with a brush over a black ground, called "peony brushwork," is representative of the kiln's output.

106

107 Large plate. Himematsu stoneware, iron glaze with finger designs. 20th century. D. 60 cm.

The Himematsu kiln in Miyagi Prefecture has been in operation barely fifteen years but produces lively everyday utensils using only local clay and glazes. In 1989 and again in 1990, the kiln took top honors at the annual exhibition of new works at the Japan Folk Crafts Museum. This large plate, one of the prize-winning works, is brimming with rugged strength.

107

Shōji Hamada

108 Large bowl. Stoneware, iron glaze dripped over white ground. 1963. D. 58 cm.
109 Flask. Stoneware, iron glaze. 1958. H. 22.3 cm.
110 Flask. Stoneware, overglaze enamels. 1935. H. 20.8 cm.

Shōji Hamada (1894–1978) was born in Kawasaki City, Kanagawa Prefecture. In 1913 he entered the Tokyo Institute of Technology, where he studied ceramics under Hazan Itaya and became acquainted with Kanjirō Kawai. After graduation he went to work at the Kyoto Ceramic Testing Institute, where Kawai was already employed, and together they studied glazing techniques. In 1918 he met Bernard Leach and visited Leach's studio at Sōetsu Yanagi's home in Chiba Prefecture. This was Hamada's first encounter with Yanagi, who was to become a lifelong friend.

In 1920 Hamada accompanied Leach to England, where they set up a kiln in the harbor town of St. Ives, Cornwall. Hamada held his first one-man show in 1923 at the Patterson Gallery in London. Returning to Japan the following year, he settled in Mashiko, Tochigi Prefecture, where with Yanagi and Kawai he became involved in the Mingei Movement.

A collector of folkcraft products from all over the world, Hamada was able to absorb the essence of each item and incorporate it skillfully into his own work. For example, the shapes of the flasks in Plates 109 and 110 are derived from Korean pottery. Hamada traveled extensively to study pottery techniques, and he was particularly fond of Okinawa. Plate 110 was made in an Okinawan kiln using local clay and glaze; the red design is extremely vibrant and beautiful. The stylized representation of Okinawan sugar millets seen in Plate 109 became one of Hamada's favored motifs. Plate 108 is a fine example of the drip glaze at which Hamada excelled and may be considered representative of his best work. Hamada was designated a Living National Treasure in 1955. In 1962 he succeeded Sōetsu Yanagi as the second director of the Japan Folk Crafts Museum, and in 1968 he was awarded the Order of Culture.

108

109 110

Kanjirō Kawai

111 Teacup. Stoneware, underglaze copper red. 1949. H. 11 cm.
112 Plaque. Stoneware. c. 1950. 35.5 x 24 cm.

Kanjirō Kawai (1890–1966) was born in Yasugi, Shimane Prefecture. In 1910 he entered the Ceramics Department of the Tokyo Institute of Technology, and after graduating he went to work as an engineer at the Kyoto Ceramic Testing Institute, where he did scientific research on ceramics. This extensive training eventually made him a respected authority on glazes. In 1920 Kawai set up his own kiln in Gojōzaka, Kyoto, and became an independent potter. He put his technical education to good use, making a stunning debut with works of true classical beauty that displayed his mastery of difficult techniques. His friendship with Sōetsu Yanagi, however, soon led him to take a radically different approach.

Kawai met Yanagi in 1924 through Shōji Hamada and formed a close relationship with him. Awakened to the beauty of folk wares, he joined Yanagi and Hamada in founding the Mingei Movement, which stressed the beauty of everyday, utilitarian objects. Kawai's own ceramics moved from the highly elaborate style of his early works to a sturdy, robust style aiming for a balance between utility and beauty.

Kawai's mature work is noted for its original, varied shapes and colorful glazes. The plaque in Plate 112 was one of Kawai's favorites, and its design of flower and hand is poetic in spirit. The use of red is particularly beautiful in the teacup in Plate 111, showing Kawai's skill with salt glaze. The floral design, hand-drawn using the *tsutsugaki* technique, is vibrant and powerful.

Kawai's creativity reached new heights in his later years, and he produced works of great variety and novelty. His reputation abroad soared too; in 1937 he won the grand prix at the Paris Exposition, and again in 1957 at the Milan Triennale International Ceramics Exhibition.

In 1920 Leach returned to England with Hamada, and together they founded a pottery-making center in St. Ives, Cornwall. From then on he was active internationally. He went to Japan eleven times, serving as an important link between East and West. While traveling around Japan, he studied and worked at various kilns.

Plate 113 is a representative work from Leach's early period, made in imitation of old slip ware. The lively rabbit design shows Leach's genius for painting. The linear decoration around the edge of the plate and the name were applied using soft clay squeezed through a cone, a method known as *tsutsugaki*.

Plates 115 and 116 were fired at the Kutani kiln in Kanazawa. Each plate uses local clay and glaze to excellent advantage, and bears Leach's inimitable stamp. His works are prized for their free, relaxed lines, exemplified by Plate 114.

111

112

113

115

114

116

Bernard Leach

113 Plate. Slipware. 1918. D. 33.3 cm.
114 Oval plate. Stoneware, galena glaze. 1953. 33.7 x 25.7 cm.
115, 116 Square plates. Porcelain, overglaze enamels. 1954. 15.6 x 15.6 cm each.

Bernard Leach (1887–1979) was born in Hong Kong and spent his early boyhood in Japan. In 1909 he met Kōtarō Takamura, then studying in London, and was stimulated to come to Japan, where he supported himself by teaching copper lithography to members of the Shirakaba literary society. One day he was invited to a tea ceremony, and the Raku ware used left a deep impression on him. Together with Kenkichi Tomimoto, he began to study with the potter Kenzan VI, and entered upon a new career. Leach also became friends with Sōetsu Yanagi, Kanjirō Kawai, and Shōji Hamada, paving the way for the development of the Mingei Movement.

WOOD

118 Lidded box. Lacquered wood. 17th century. W. 49 x D. 45.6 x H. 32 cm.

After lacquer was applied to this box, gold foil was inlaid to form a design of butterbur leaves. The box's original function is unclear, but on the reverse side are cords for carrying. Perhaps peddlars placed their most valuable merchandise in it, or perhaps a daimyo retainer carried it for his lord. In any case, the excellence of the design indicates that whatever it held must have been precious.

119 Chest (*tansu*). Wood, with iron fittings. 19th century. H. 94 x W. 70 x D. 36 cm.

The Hokuriku area is known for its fine zelkova wood chests with wrought iron fittings. This chest was specially made for indoor use by a craftsman of sea chests. Since it is stacked in two units and has many small drawers, it was probably a case for account books. Shops prized fine chests like this one, which conveyed an aura of prestige.

120 Sea chest (*funa-dansu*). Wood, with iron fittings. 18th century. H. 47.5 x W. 42 x D. 51 cm.

Among the many chests made in Japan, sea chests (*funa-dansu*) are particularly deserving of note. They were securely outfitted with metal trim, like warriors fortified for battle. And just as some warriors wore fancy armor, many chests were decorated with elaborate metalwork fittings.

Sea chests were placed aboard large trading ships and used as safes to guard money as well as important documents that had to be kept dry. On long voyages, captains stored personal effects in them as well. Such chests had to be as heavy and sturdy as possible to withstand the pitching and rolling of rough seas. (*Kōgei* [Craftwork], 1933.)

121 Pipe holder and tobacco containers. Cherry bark. 20th century. Containers: W. 8.5 x D. 3.2 x H. 10.3 cm; W. 8.5 x D. 3.5 x H. 8.3 cm. Pipe holder: L. 24.5 cm.

122 Box. Cherry bark. 20th century. W. 30 x D. 39 x H. 17 cm.

These objects are all handcrafted from wild cherry bark (*kabazaiku*) and owe their distinctive character to this wood's special properties. First, cherry bark has a subdued reddish-purple color. Second, it has a beautiful luster, and shines like lacquer when polished. Third, it is extremely tough; sideways it tears easily, but vertically it is nearly indestructible. (*Kōgei* [Craftwork], No. 120, 1942.)

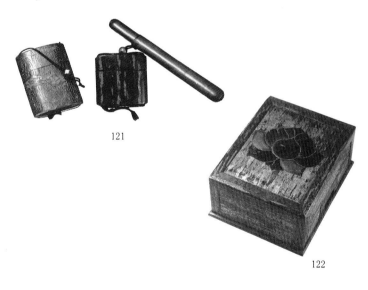

123 Kitchen talisman. Wood. 19th century. 60 x 39 cm.

The area in northeastern Japan where Akita, Iwate, and Miyagi Prefectures converge remains even now a relatively inaccessible, unexplored part of the country. A product of this region is this kitchen mask (*kamado men*), designed to be hung over a cooking area. When a new house was built, it was customary for the master carpenter or plasterer to make a mask to be attached to the pillar closest to the kitchen in order to ward off evil. People strove to make masks of sufficient strength to overcome malevolent spirits. Only when the talismanic mask was fastened to the pillar was the house considered to be finished.

123

124 Lion headdress. Lacquered wood. 18th century. 22 x 18 x 19.5 cm.

This headdress in the shape of a lion's head was part of a costume worn by performers of a ceremonial lion dance (*shishi-mai*). This dance was popular throughout Japan, and consequently such heads were produced by craftsmen in all regions. (*Mingei Zukan* [Encyclopedia of Folkcrafts], 1960.)

124

125 Carp-shaped crosspiece of pot hanger. Wood. W. 35.5 cm.
127 *Noshi*-shaped crosspiece of pot hanger. Wood. 18th century. W. 38.5 cm.
Fan-shaped crosspiece of pot hanger. Wood. 18th century. W. 34 cm.

The horizontal crosspieces for *jizai*, which traditionally hung suspended over the hearth, were made of zelkova wood. Like *jizaikake*, they were usually carved into shapes with auspicious meanings or suggestive of water. The examples shown here—*noshi* (the label attached to gifts), a fan, and a carp—indicate the range of objects carved. These crosspieces are all products of the Hokuriku area (Toyama, Fukui, and Ishikawa Prefectures). (*Nihon no Mingei* [Japanese Folkcrafts], 1960.)

126 Pot hanger (*jizaikake*). Wood. 19th century. 40 x 48 cm.

Pot hangers of this shape are called Ebisu, after a folk deity often associated with kitchens. Unlike the Daikoku style (Plate 128), there is no overlying cap. The apparatus for suspending cooking pots over the hearth hung from hangers such as this. One often comes across blocks of natural wood used for this purpose, but this example from the Hokuriku area (Toyama, Fukui, and Ishikawa Prefectures) has been carved into a hook shape. Made of zelkova wood, it is extremely heavy. The dark black patina is indicative of its long history. (*Kōgei* [Craftwork], No. 3, 1931.)

127 See note for Plate 125.

128 Pot hanger (*jizaikake*). Wood. 19th century. 40 x 44 cm.

This style of hanger is usually known as Daikoku, after the god of wealth (another tutelary deity of the kitchen) who is usually depicted wearing a black hat. This is the most common shape for pot hangers, with the upper part in the shape of a Chinese character. The straight lines of the top balance perfectly with the roundness of the bottom. The inset lines on this hanger indicate that it was well used. It was originally lacquered, and the color has further deepened by smoke and handling. The wood is zelkova. The small protuberances on the top are for attaching the rope. No other type of Japanese woodwork possesses such solidity and strength. (*Kōgei* [Craftwork], No. 3, 1931.)

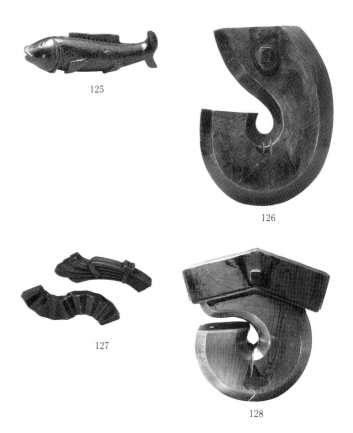

129–131 Shop signboards. Wood. 19th century. Dimensions, from left to right: 97 x 26.7 cm; 132 x 52.7 cm; 146 x 52 cm.

Commerce was thriving in castle towns and villages throughout Japan during the Edo period (1600–1868). Merchants vied with one another, hanging eye-catching signs to advertise their businesses. The signboards shown here belonged respectively to shops selling tobacco (Plate 131), brushes and ink (Plate 130), and candlesticks (Plate 129); each depicts the type of object that is for sale, thus fulfilling the basic condition for an advertising sign—namely, that it enable people to identify quickly the nature of the business, even from a distance. The messages and designs are simple and clear. For maximum visibility to passersby, signs were hung from shop eaves at right angles to the street, with the same design on front and back. Handles were attached for ease in hanging them out each morning and taking them down for storage each evening.

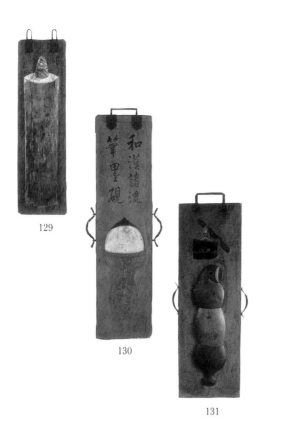

132 Handbag. Braided bamboo. 20th century. 23 x 35 cm.
134 Trunk. Braided bamboo. 19th century. 33 x 40 x 22 cm.

Japan has a rich supply of bamboo, including over 500 indigenous species. Because bamboo is smooth and lustrous, grows fast, and is light, strong, and easy to work with, it has been used in many areas of daily life since ancient times. In the warm regions of central and lower Honshū, sturdy *madake* (*Phyllostachus bambusoides*) is commonly used, while in the colder northeast regions, slender forms of bamboo prevail. Plate 134 is a traditional container for storing clothes, known commonly as a *kōri*; long years of use have given it a beautiful sheen. The handbag in Plate 132, made in Tottori Prefecture, is an example of bamboo craft adapted to the needs of modern life.

133 Pannier. Straw. 38 x 4 x 37 cm.

In the Tōhoku region one encounters a great variety of panniers known as *shoiko*, which differ according to the local materials. The one pictured here is from Akita Prefecture. The straw plaits are thick and strong. Those in the warp have been darkened with carbon black, probably to protect them from rain damage. The side panels are firmly bound with brown plant fiber. The contrast with the dark vertical wickerwork forms a natural pattern reminiscent of the woven geometric designs found in American Indian basketry. (*Mingei Zukan* [Encyclopedia of Folkcrafts], 1963.)

134 See note for Plate 132.

192 MINGEI

LACQUER

135 Lidded bowl. *Negoro* lacquer. 18th century. D. 14 cm.

Negoro refers to a type of lacquerware in which red lacquer is applied over black. Over time the red surface wears away to expose the black layers underneath. The subtle blend of red and black lends unique beauty to *negoro* lacquer utensils and reflects a distinctly Japanese aesthetic sensibility. The more this bowl is used, the more beautiful it is destined to become.

135

136 Bowl. Lacquer with gold leaf. 17th century. D. 14 cm.
137 Bowl. Lacquer with gold leaf. 17th century. D. 13.3 cm.

"Hidehira bowls" are a well-known type of lacquerware. The name is derived from Fujiwara no Hidehira (?–1187), the head of a clan that ruled the Ōshū Province of Japan in the 11th century. They were produced in or near the province of Rikuchū (present-day Iwate and Akita Prefectures). Distinctive features of such bowls are the designs painted in red lacquer. Added to this is gold leaf, cut in diamond shapes and applied along the rims of the bowls.

136

137

138 Bowl. Lacquered wood. 18th century. D. 12.8 cm.

This bowl has an especially striking black and red lacquer design, with three stacked diamond shapes resembling pine bark. While this traditional Japanese motif was used frequently in dyeing, it appears less often in lacquerware.

138

139 Hot water pitcher. Lacquered wood. 16th century. H. 26 cm.

This hot water pitcher (*yutō*) may have been used at a large temple complex. The striking combination of red and black lacquer is extremely modern in sensibility. Such a work is at once old and new.

139

140 Vase. Lacquered wood. 16th century. H. 30 cm.

This lacquer vase was originally used in religious ceremonies. Its elegantly simple shape has been enhanced by the addition of oak (*kashiwa*) leaf designs rendered with red and black lacquer. Painting with raw lacquer mixed with pigment is exceedingly difficult. Nevertheless, here the motifs have been rendered skillfully and harmoniously. (*Mingei Zukan* [Encyclopedia of Folkcrafts], 1960.)

140

NOTES TO THE PLATES   193

141 Spouted bowl. Lacquered wood. 17th century. D. 20.5 cm.

This is a splendid example of lacquerware decorated with inlaid gold leaf (*hakuoki*). It was produced in the northern provinces of Japan, where such spouted bowls are called *hiage*. (*Nihon no Mingei* [Japanese Folkcrafts], 1960.)

141

METAL

142 Brass candlestand. 19th century. H. 29 cm.

Before the advent of electric lights in Japan, candles and linseed oil lanterns were used for light. This candlestand is equipped with a hook to hang scissors (used for trimming the wick) and a compartment to store wicks. The handle and body are well balanced for a pleasantly streamlined effect. Modern designers have much to learn from objects like this.

142

143 Brass *hibachi*. 19th century. H. 24.5 cm.

Charcoal fires were an important source of heat in Japanese homes. *Hibachi*, or charcoal braziers, were made of a variety of materials including wood, porcelain, and metal. The *hibachi* shown here has holes into which handles can be fitted for ease in transporting. The overall design is simple and beautiful and exemplifies the principle, seen throughout folkcraft, that devotion to utility leads to simplification of form.

143

144 Brass caldron. 19th century. H. 28.5 cm.

Japan has a long history of metalworking, during which forms were refined and perfected. This brass caldron has very clean lines. The lid and wide brim are also beautiful. It was not designed to hang above a hearth, but to be used for cooking over an earthen furnace called a *kudo*.

144

145 Brass kettle. 19th century. H. 29 cm.

This brass kettle has a magnificent flared skirt shape. When hung over a fire, it conducts heat efficiently so that water would boil quickly. Conversely, the thick handle is hollow, making it cooler for carrying purposes. It is the product of wisdom culled over long years.

145

146 Iron kettle. 19th century. H. 21.5 cm.

This kettle was made to hang over the fire in a traditional Japanese house. Used in the preparation of tea, such vessels were indispensable articles in daily life, and owners took justifiable pride in them. The surface of this kettle is covered with small milletlike protuberances; unlike the refined works belonging to the upper classes, it has a powerful strength suggestive of the sturdiness of farmers themselves.

146

PICTORIAL ART

147 *View of Edo Bay Fortifications.* *Doro-e.* Gouache on paper. 19th century. 88 x 235 cm.

148 *View of Western Castle.* *Doro-e.* Gouache on paper. 19th century. 37 x 52.5 cm.

149 *View of Kinokuni Slope.* *Doro-e.* Gouache on paper. 19th century. 24 x 33 cm.

Doro-e (literally, "mud pictures") form a special genre of paintings by Japanese painters and scholars of the Edo period (1600–1868). They incorporate Western painting techniques, which were introduced by the Italian missionary Mateo Ricci to China and by Dutchmen residing in Nagasaki, then Japan's only window to the outside world. The technique of one-point perspective captured the fancy of Japanese artists and was used extensively in *doro-e*, as was chiaroscuro shading.

147

148

149

150 Stone rubbing of Buddhist deity. Ink on paper. 82.3 x 35.3 cm.

Walking along the Shinano Road in Nagano Prefecture, one comes across all sorts of stone Buddhas and folk deities at the side of the road or ensconced in small shrines. Now they are abandoned, left to the mercies of wind and rain, but not long ago they were the objects of devout faith. Some are as old as the Kamakura period (1185–1333), but more often they date from the Edo period

(1600–1868). The faces of the older images are more forbidding and devoid of softness. The Blue-faced Kongō was one of the most commonly depicted Buddhist deities. Faith in this god was believed to protect against sickness. (*Mingei Zukan* [Encyclopedia of Folkcrafts], 1960.)

150

151 Stone rubbing of roadside folk deities. Ink on paper. 55.2 x 50.4 cm.

Japanese folk religion is a blend of Shinto and Buddhist beliefs, with additional influences from Confucianism and Taoism. The variety of legends and customs in different parts of the country gave folk religion a particularly colorful character. A ubiquitous manifestation of folk beliefs were *dōsojin*, deities worshipped in the form of stone images placed along the roadside. These images have long been the focus of scholarly attention, and many are worthy of consideration as works of art. Shinshū (present-day Nagano Prefecture) is a particularly rich source of them. In this rubbing a man and woman are portrayed hand in hand, symbolizing a wish for marital happiness. (*Mingei Zukan* [Encyclopedia of Folkcrafts], 1960.)

151

152 *Benkei*. Ōtsu-e. Ink and color on paper. 18th century. 53.5 x 22.7 cm.
153 *Monkey, Catfish, and Gourd*. Ōtsu-e. Ink and color on paper. 18th century. 53.5 x 22 cm.

Frontispiece *Wisteria Maiden*. Ōtsu-e. Ink and color on paper. 18th century. 61.5 x 22.3 cm.

In addition to paintings by famous artists patronized by kings, aristocrats, or other wealthy individuals, in every culture there have also been paintings by unknown artists depicting the beliefs and pleasures of common people. Pictures treating religious themes began to be sold in large numbers during the Kan'ei era (1624–44) at roadside stands in Oiwake, near Ōtsu on the old Tōkaidō Road linking Edo with Kyoto and Osaka. Roughly drawn on poor-quality paper, these cheap pictures by unknown artists—called Ōtsu-e (Ōtsu pictures)—are representative of folk painting in Japan. By the end of the Genroku era (1688–1704), Ōtsu-e portrayed not only religious themes, but also popular subjects such as dancers, famous beauties, and the like. Many were rendered satirically, expressing a humorous attitude toward contemporary life and toward political and religious authorities.

The three examples here are the Wisteria Maiden (Fuji-musume), a female dancer holding wisteria bunches; Benkei, a legendary warrior-monk who valiantly supported the Minamoto clan; and a foolish monkey trying to capture a slippery catfish with a gourd. Each one demonstrates the beauty, power, and humor of the Ōtsu-e genre. In the process of producing large numbers of these paintings at a fast pace, the style was abbreviated and the paintings took on the qualities of mass-produced art. The unrestrained brushwork and vivid colors add life to the paintings.

152

153

Keisuke Serizawa

154 *Papermaking Village.* Stencil-dyed cotton. 73.5 x 66 cm.
155 *Ryūkyū Scene.* Stencil-dyed cotton. 63.5 x 80 cm.
156 *Straw Cape.* Stencil-dyed cotton. 207 x 94.5 cm.

Textile designer and dyer Keisuke Serizawa (1895–1976) studied design in industrial art school. At the age of 31, he encountered Sōetsu Yanagi's article "Kōgei no Michi" (The Way of Crafts) and became an adherent of Yanagi's theory of beauty, applying it in the field of textiles. He accompanied Yanagi on a tour of Okinawa in 1938, where he discovered a traditional method of stencil dyeing called *bingatazome*. Serizawa studied, mastered, and then adapted this craft to his own ends, creating a form of art called *katazome-e*. In 1956 he was designated a Living National Treasure for his work in preserving *bingatazome* and developing it into an art form. A consummately gifted artist, Serizawa portrayed a rich variety of subjects—the changing seasons, flowers and birds, annual events, ceremonies, scenes and manners, lifestyles, and objects of daily use.

The works here are all examples of stencil dyeing (*katazome*). *Papermaking Village* (Plate 154) is a study in symmetry. A single stencil was used to dye one half of the picture, then turned over and used again for the other half. At the top of the picture are green mountains and a stream, while the lower part depicts a peaceful scene of paper-making, where sheets of handcrafted paper (*washi*) have been spread on boards to dry in the sun.

Ryūkyū Scene (Plate 155) shows a marketplace in premodern Okinawa (Ryūkyū). Serizawa vividly depicted the appearance and manners of people wandering through the market using the bright, cheerful colors of the south.

Plate 156 depicts a type of straw cape (*mino*) worn by farmers in northern Honshu; the actual cape is in the possession of the Japan Folk Crafts Museum. The red and white of the collar and sash form a striking contrast against the subdued colors and heavily textured rendition of the straw.

154

155

156

Shikō Munakata

157 *In Praise of the Tōhoku District.* Woodcuts, from a pair of six-fold screens. 1937. Dimensions from left to right: 117 x 111 cm., 120.5 x 74 cm., 121 x 117 cm. Size of screen: 183 x 1028 cm.
158 *Goddesses of Heaven and Earth.* Ink and color on paper. 1954. 125 x 164 cm.

Shikō Munakata (1903–75) was born in the Tsugaru region of northern Honshu, the son of a poor blacksmith who made farming implements. He decided he wanted to be a painter at an early age; art school was beyond his means, but he devoted much of his spare time to sketching. In the 1930s he came across reproductions of works by Impressionist painters and was particularly attracted to Van Gogh. Later he encountered woodcuts and taught himself the art by trial and error. In 1936 he submitted a woodcut entitled *Yamato shi uruwashi* (How beautiful is Yamato), based on a tale from ancient Japanese mythology, to a public art exhibition organized by leading Japanese artists. The work promptly attracted the attention of Sōetsu Yanagi, Shōji Hamada, and Kanjirō Kawai, who subsequently purchased it. Before long, Munakata had joined them in their commitment to the Mingei Movement.

Munakata's woodcuts reflect his remarkable creativity and artistic imagination. He was able to capture the essence of the forces of nature and the doings of mankind, and to express these things in his own powerful way. His work combines a strong attachment to the customs and folklore of the area where he was born, rare among modern city-dwellers, with deeply religious feelings and veneration for his ancestors and for the past.

In Praise of the Tōhoku District (Plate 157), an early masterpiece, is part of an extremely large work composed of some 120 separate woodcuts. The Tōhoku area where Munakata was born is a cold, impoverished region where people are patient and warmhearted. The central figure in this work is a local deity, with children on either side of him symbolizing life.

Goddesses of Heaven and Earth (Plate 158) shows two naked women running with great energy. Female figures appear frequently in Munakata's works, including those with religious themes. For Munakata women symbolized procreation and life. In this painting of two women representing heaven and earth, Munakata offers his personal vision of the mystery of the cosmos and the vibrant energy of life.

157

158

Acknowledgments

Glasgow Museums would like to thank the following individuals and organizations for their help and assistance in the overall project:

Dr. Sōri Yanagi, Director of the Japan Folk Crafts Museum (Mingei-kan), and the team of curators headed by Mr. Junichi Sasaki, for making the final selection of items for display and for planning much of the exhibition's design; Nick Pearce, Assistant Keeper (Oriental Art) at The Burrell Collection, and Mrs. Teiko Utsumi, Project Director at the Japan Folk Crafts Museum, for making all the detailed arrangements concerning the exhibition and its UK tour and this publication; Ambassador Toshio Yamazaki, Deputy Chairman of the Japan Festival Committee, Japan, and Sir Hugh Cortazzi, Vice-Chairman, Japan Festival Committee, UK, for their support; Yasuo Harada, Deputy Executive Secretary of the Japan office, for his effort; Joe Earle, Exhibitions Co-ordinator of the Japan Festival, for all his very active assistance; Yutaka Seki, photographer, for his exquisite camera work; Pat Fister, of the Spencer Museum of Art, University of Kansas, for her editorial assistance with the text.

In addition we acknowledge the support of Glasgow Museums curatorial, and corporate services staff; Mr. Neil Sinclair, Group Museums Officer, and Dr. Juliet Horsley, Museums Officer (Fine and Applied Art) at Sunderland Museum and Art Gallery; at the Crafts Council, Ms. Linda Theophilus, Head of Exhibitions. Finally, Barry Lancet and Shigeyoshi Suzuki at Kodansha International for their invaluable contribution toward producing this splendid book.